DECOLONIZE YOUR DIET

DECOLONIZE
YOUR DIET

Plant-Based Mexican-American Recipes for Health and Healing

LUZ CALVO & CATRIONA RUEDA ESQUIBEL

Arsenal Pulp Press ✦ *Vancouver*

DECOLONIZE YOUR DIET

Copyright © 2015 by Luz Calvo and Catriona Rueda Esquibel

FOURTH PRINTING: 2017

ARSENAL PULP PRESS
Suite 202–211 East Georgia St.
Vancouver, BC V6A 1Z6
Canada
arsenalpulp.com

The author and publisher assert that the information contained
in this book is true and complete to the best of their knowledge.
All recommendations are made without the guarantee on the
part of the author and publisher. The author and publisher dis-
claim any liability in connection with the use of this information.
For more information, contact the publisher.

Note for our UK readers: measurements for non-liquids are for
volume, not weight.

Design by Gerilee McBride
All photographs, prop styling, and food styling by
    Tracey Kusiewicz / Foodie Photography
Cover illustration: "Maíz Sagrado" by Veronica Perez
Editing by Susan Safyan

Printed and bound in Korea

Library and Archives Canada Cataloguing in Publication:
Calvo, Luz, 1960–, author
    Decolonize your diet : plant-based Mexican-American
recipes for health and healing / Luz Calvo & Catriona Rueda
Esquibel.

Includes index.
Issued in print and electronic formats.
ISBN 978-1-55152-592-1 (paperback).
—ISBN 978-1-55152-593-8 (epub)

    1. Vegetarian cooking. 2. Mexican American cooking. 3.
Plants, Edible—Health aspects. 4. Cookbooks. I. Esquibel,
Catrióna Rueda, 1965–, author II. Title.

TX837.C34 2015   641.5'636
C2015-903460-4

                                              C2015-903461-2

With our heart in our hands and our hands in the soil...

CONTENTS

FOREWORD

From the first page to the last, it is clear that Luz Calvo and Catriona Rueda Esquibel's book is motivated by love: their love for each other, for their communities, for the delicious food of their ancestors, and for our planet. Their plant-forward recipes explore the healthiest aspects of Mexican cuisine. I see *Decolonize Your Diet* as a playful mix of cultural reclamation, food politics, and vegetarian recipes. Some of the recipes are classic healthy dishes that have always been a mainstay of Mexican cuisine—a slow-cooked pot of beans or a zesty cactus salad. In others, Luz and Catriona bring their farm-to-table sensibility to traditional dishes such as their Tortillas Smothered in Pumpkin Mole (p. 124) or Red Pozole with Medicinal Mushrooms (p. 101). Other recipes are creative reconfigurations of pre-Conquest ingredients or dishes, such as their Tacos de mi Corazón (p. 137)—made from stewed hearts of palm—or their outrageously delicious chocolate tamales (Xocolatamal, p. 193).

I am enthusiastic about *Decolonize Your Diet* because its mission so closely reflects my own. In *Afro-Vegan*, I focus on farm-fresh, Afro-diasporic fare and share the rich and often painful histories of people of African descent as expressed through food. As I travel the country giving talks, I have encountered Latinas and Latinos who appreciate my work and want to apply a similar approach to their own cooking practice. I always refer them to Luz and Catriona. Drawing from their research on traditional Mesoamerican cuisine, they demonstrate the ways that home-cooked meals carry history, memory, and stories, and connect contemporary Latinas/os to their ancestors. Along with my own work, *Decolonize Your Diet* is part of a larger movement utilizing ancestral knowledge to help communities of color respond to the public health crises and the decimation of our food system's foundation, brought upon us by the industrialized, Western diet. Our collective goal is to empower people to choose wholesome foods to improve the physical and spiritual health of our families, communities, and Mother Earth. I invite you to sample the flavors of pre-Conquest Mexico as you join us in the project of decolonizing our diets.

—Bryant Terry, James Beard Foundation Leadership Award recipient and author of Afro-Vegan: Farm-Fresh African, Caribbean, and Southern Flavors Remixed

Libradita Tafoya Esquibel with her youngest children and a granddaughter. Northern New Mexico, 1952

INTRODUCTION

The recovery of the people is tied to the recovery of food, since food itself is medicine, not only for the body, but for the soul, and for the spiritual connection.
—Winona LaDuke

In Catriona's Words

My father Alfonso describes growing up in rural, northern New Mexico in the 1940s and '50s. The family enjoyed a diverse diet ensured by the labor of his mother, Libradita Tafoya Esquibel. Her kitchen garden produced squash and other vegetables. She gathered wild greens and herbs and cooked seasonal Lenten dishes to accommodate the family's ritual abstinence from meat. She put up summer's fruit for winter eating. She made thick, bready white flour tortillas and raised baby chicks next to her stove every year to provide eggs and meat for her family. When my grandmother left her abusive marriage and went to live with her grown daughters in Colorado, my dad's world changed dramatically. Without my grandmother's unpaid labor to provide a healthy diet, my father and the remaining family members could afford only the cheapest, most easily prepared meals, most often canned foods. Eventually, my father's family migrated to Colorado, then Wyoming, and finally Los Angeles. Most of the members of my father's generation developed type 2 diabetes as adults.

When Luz and I started to get to know each other in 1995, food was always part of the scene: I brought my vegetarian pozole to Luz's potluck. The first "date dinner" I cooked for Luz was New Mexico Green

Chile Stew (p. 96). Those two, along with my red chile tofu enchiladas, were the only "from scratch" meals I knew how to make. After we moved in together in 1996, my sister emailed me her mother-in-law's recipe so we could cook homemade flour tortillas together. Our song was the classic "Sabor a Mí."

The next nine years took us all over the country, from Santa Cruz, California (where we met as graduate students), to Las Cruces, New Mexico (my first job, while Luz wrote a dissertation and trained to run a marathon), to Columbus, Ohio (Luz's first tenure-track gig). In Las Cruces, the summers were so hot that we had to learn new ways of cooking and eating. Luz would cook first thing in the morning and then chill the foods so we could have a cold salad for dinner. Pasta salad, rice salad, bean salad: we had a whole repertoire of recipe ideas that we could plan our shopping and meals around. In Ohio, we had the perfect little kitchen, set up so that I could play sous chef and chop on one side of the counter while Luz spun and sautéed and played master chef on the other side. In 2005, we moved back to northern California when we got our current jobs at Cal State East Bay and San Francisco State University, and we thought we could finally catch our breath, now that we were home again. One of the first things we did was buy a lemon tree. Luz planted it in a big pot, and we cared for it on our deck. The lemon tree was a symbol of our happy return to California.

The following spring, Luz was diagnosed with breast cancer, and our world changed dramatically. During chemo, Luz had absolutely no appetite and lost twenty pounds. My own eating became solitary and secretive. We were completely off-balance. My work colleagues got together and gifted us a year of organic grocery delivery, and Luz's colleagues brought us meals. One book that helped us a lot was Rebecca Katz's *One Bite at a Time*, not so much because it had recipes that became our favorites but because she gave us a way of thinking about food. Katz's recipes are built around F.A.S.S.: Fat, Acid, Salt, Sweet. She says those four flavors are what make food taste good. And so even if you can only stomach a tiny meal, those flavors need to be there. After Luz completed treatment, food was no longer something to be enjoyed; it was something to be feared, something that could bring back the cancer. That's why our garden and eventually our chickens, became so important to our food life: it was one small area where we had control. We knew the kind of lives our chickens had lived, and we saw them racing around happily in the yard. Luz learned square-foot gardening and permaculture food-matchmaking (tomatoes love basil, and strawberries love chives). Our neighbor across the backyard gave us a rue plant, *ruda*, for memory and for spiritual protection. He was a Holocaust survivor who had grown up on the Isle of Rhodes, and he grew hundreds of plants in pots, some of them breaking through the bottoms of their pots and setting roots into the

ground. He was always talking to Luz over the fence and sharing seeds he had collected.

In Mexican healing traditions there's a condition called *susto*, a fright, which startles the spirit from the body. One of the ways of treating this is to cover a person's body with soil, to reconnect them to the earth, to this life. For Luz, working in our garden turned out to be the treatment for the *susto* that settled in after the cancer diagnosis, and growing our own food brought us to realize that food can give life, bring strength. My *susto* was that my Luz would be taken away from me. I didn't want to have to be the strong one: I wanted to sing sobbing Mexican songs "*El sol sin luz nunca es sol/el mar sin agua no es mar/y yo sin ti no soy nada*" ("The sun without light is no sun/the sea without water is no sea/and I, without you, I am nothing"). My dad came to visit us and showed us how to break up and remove the concrete from our backyard so Luz could build more raised beds and expand the garden. I put in an irrigation system, we composted our chicken manure with our food waste, and made rich black soil. And we learned to live again in our bodies and on this earth.

There's a saying among cancer survivors that as they adjust to "the new normal," from being in crisis-mode to finding their way through every day, that they are at last able to move from buying only ripe bananas to being able to buy green bananas again. It's about

trusting that they will be there for the fruit to ripen. Alongside our raised beds, Luz started tearing up more concrete and planted fruit trees. I wrote this poem:

> love is in the garden
> with the chickens
> in the herb spiral
> transplanting the lemon tree
> setting down roots

In Luz's Words

In 2006, when I was diagnosed with breast cancer, I was stunned. I had been a vegetarian for fifteen years, and I considered myself to be very healthy. The entire year after diagnosis was consumed by treatment, surgery, chemotherapy, and emotion. Catriona became my caretaker, and she was a total trooper: She took me to appointments, took careful notes on what the cancer doctors told us, did the shopping, and cooked for me as best she could. Since I am the cook in our family, the whole world felt upside down. I was completely depleted. My spirit, usually strong, was barely there. With the diagnosis, time stopped as all my energy went to dealing with the treatments and to the basics of survival. Eventually, as I started to re-emerge, I turned to research to answer the questions that were racing through my mind: Why me? Where did I go wrong? What can I do to survive this?

Codex Osuna, folio 38 "Herb Gatherer"

My research led me to some interesting findings about breast cancer in Latina/o communities. First, I found that Mexico has some of the lowest rates of breast cancer in the world. Second, I found a study published in 2005 that looked at breast cancer rates among Latinas in the San Francisco Bay area where we lived. This study found that immigrant Latinas had significantly lower rates of breast cancer than US-born Latinas. Moreover, the longer Latina immigrants lived in the US, the higher their risk for developing breast cancer. Also, curiously, learning English was associated with a higher risk of breast cancer among the immigrant women. I started thinking about these findings and wondered what accounted for the differences. Something in the US and something about acculturating to US culture were likely contributing to these increased breast cancer rates. As I continued my research, I found that these statistics extended beyond breast cancer, and were also true for many other diseases and health concerns. And that's when a light went on for me. What if the diet of rural Mexico and Central America, a diet that is ancestral and plant-based (beans, corn, squash, wild greens, nopales [prickly pear cactus], fresh fruit, nuts, and seeds) was protecting folks from the diseases associated with life in the US, such as diabetes, heart disease, and some cancers?

With this new theory, we started to research the health benefits of certain ancestral Mexican and Central American foods. We started to evaluate Mesoamerican cuisine and quickly found that foods from the pre-Hispanic era (i.e., before colonization) were among the healthiest foods on the planet and that many of the less healthy aspects of Mesoamerican cuisine came about as a direct result of colonization—with the introduction of wheat, beef, cheese, cooking oils, and sugar. Before colonization, Mesoamerican food was steamed, grilled or cooked on a clay skillet known as a *comal*. Meat was eaten only in small quantities. Our ancestors gathered and ate wild herbs and greens. They cultivated hundreds of different varieties of beans, squash, and corn, not just the few varieties now available at most grocery stores. In terms of corn, in particular, our ancestors created a rich and sustaining cuisine that included yellow, white, red, blue, and black corn, made tamales (p. 143 for Butternut Squash & Roasted Green Chile Tamalitos), tacos (p. 133 for Hibiscus Flower Tacos), atoles (p. 103 for Healing Green Chileatole), tlacoyos (p. 138 for Tlacoyos con Nopales), and more.

Thus began our quest to decolonize our diet. First, we started eating simple foods: a fresh pot of beans! And then I learned how to make fresh corn tortillas from scratch. Ah! My spirit awoke. I recalled warm memories of these tastes and smells from childhood. We decided to raise our own chickens. I started a garden and found seeds for wild greens like *quelites* (lamb's quarters) and *verdolagas* (purslane). With the help of friends, we

liberated paved spaces so that we could plant fruit trees. In the center of the garden, I constructed an herb spiral where I grow many herbs, including Mesoamerican species, like Mexican oregano, *pipicha (Porophyllum linaria)* *pápalo (Porophyllum ruderale)* and lemon verbena. The very act of clearing land, touching the soil with my bare hands, and planting seeds worked to re-ground my spirit. My first homemade taco *de quelites* was a revelation, connecting me to my grandmother Luz, who had spoken fondly of eating these wild greens in her native state of Sonora in northern Mexico. We worked for several years on (re)educating ourselves about these foods. I grew stronger, and Catriona was a willing participant in my garden and food experiments: tasting, offering encouragement and appreciation, and making sure the kitchen was clean and well stocked. Over time, my fear and anxiety about the cancer were replaced with gratitude (not about the cancer, not ever), but about our newfound connections to Mother Earth, to our ancestors, to ancestral knowledge, to our own spirits, and to the new post-cancer life Catriona and I were building together.

Recipes to Sustain Revolutionary Love

Our project was born out of both struggle and love, both personal and political. *Decolonize Your Diet* begins with the premise that we are living with the legacy of over 500 years of colonization of the Americas.

Throughout the Americas, colonization meant the transfer of land from Native peoples to Europeans, the death of millions of indigenous people, rape of Native women, and the violent suppression of indigenous languages, religions, and cultures. We recognize the importance of indigenous knowledge, cultures, and ways of being in the world and believe in the need to dismantle colonial systems of power and knowledge.

For us, helping to build an awareness of the relationship between food and community offers one way to reclaim indigenous knowledge. We are writing a cookbook, but not just for individual cooks to read, or even cook from, while isolated in their kitchens. The project of decolonizing our diets cannot be accomplished through *individual* acts of food preparation. Instead, we hope that our project will inspire our readers to think critically about the effects of colonization on the food we eat and motivate them to get involved in their communities. We encourage our readers to act collectively to create a world in which everyone—from the residents of US urban food deserts, to farmworkers, to small farmers—has access to organic, wholesome, ancestral foods that are grown in ways that respect the delicate ecosystems of our planet.

Politically, as Chicanas/os, we believe it is important to stand in solidarity with our native brothers, sisters, and trans siblings across our continent. As citizens

WHAT KIND OF ANCESTOR

WILL YOU BE?

QUE TIPO DE ANCESTRO SERAS?

WHAT ABOUT THE SEVENTH GENERATION? WHAT WILL THEY HAVE?

*Florentine Codex, volume 5,
chapter 4 "Woman Speaking a
Blessing over Corn"*

of the US and Canada, we understand that we have a responsibility to contest the immense power of US and Canadian governments and multinational corporations, who are wreaking havoc on native communities: displacing people, polluting lands and waterways, and threatening ancestral seeds. We are living in the midst of a huge battle waged by multinational corporations that aim to control the seed supply through seed patents and genetically modified organisms (GMOs). It is within these broader contexts that we issue the call to "decolonize your diet," with full knowledge that what we need is a dismantling of our entire food-for-profit system.

Another mission of this book is to encourage individuals in our communities to use food in order to regain physical health and nurture a spiritual connection to themselves, each other, and Mother Earth. When we say food is medicine, it is not because we think food can necessarily replace other conventional Western medical treatments, but because eating "real" food is essential to healing. Many of us have become disconnected from this truth and, therefore, from our own bodies.

Cooking a pot of beans from scratch is a revolutionary act that honors both our ancestors and future generations. We have learned from our First Nation (Iroquois) comrades the concept of honoring the

seven generations that came before us and the seven generations that come after us. We believe that food is a nexus connecting the generations. These spiritual values speak to human physiology as well. The emerging field of epigenetics has found that the foods our grandparents ate and the toxins to which they were exposed can have a direct bearing on our own health. When Luz was interviewed for a study on Latina breast cancer, the researcher asked if Luz's grandparents had worked in the fields. (They had.) When Luz asked why that was relevant, the researcher explained that environment can change a person's genes and those genetic changes can be passed on to subsequent generations. In the case of farmworkers, exposure to pesticides and toxins may actually change the genes that are passed on. We believe that what you eat now, what you put in your body, can have genetic consequences for future generations.

For us, spirituality is about connecting each of us to our common humanity, to our ancestors, to our elders, to our youth, to our earth, and to a larger purpose. It is vital to honor and respect the cultural and spiritual aspects of food. We believe that humans, animals, and plants have spirits. When we eat, we connect to the spiritual essence of what we ingest. When we eat traditional foods, we connect to our ancestors. We think it is important to have gratitude for the food we eat as we are eating it—to be mindful of all the sacrifices

that went into having food on our table. Rather than disavowing the lives, the labor, and even the suffering that produce our food, we think it is important to acknowledge this complexity and be humbled by it. We hope that as we energize our bodies and spirits with wholesome food, we also energize ourselves to continue to struggle for decolonization and food justice.

We seek to honor and reclaim the healthy aspects of our complex histories and multiple cultures. As Chicanas/os, we acknowledge the cultural mixing that forms our identities, and we embrace the work of cultural theorist, poet, and activist Gloria Anzaldúa, who urges us to live in the borderlands—neither here nor there, but in the middle. In her influential poem, "To Live in the Borderlands Means You," Anzaldúa writes of being caught between and among various races, ethnicities, languages, and cultures while eating "whole wheat tortillas." Whole wheat tortillas are a healthy alternative to white flour tortillas, but flour tortillas themselves are a product of colonization: indigenous tortillas are made from corn. Like Anzaldúa, we combine and incorporate non-native foods if they further the goal of healing our bodies and spirits. Thus, you might see non-native ingredients like carrots, beets, and cilantro in some of our recipes. We even develop a whole-wheat tortilla recipe in honor of Anzaldúa.

In general, our recipes highlight the immense diversity of healthy, native foods in dishes that are accessible, yet satisfying. Reclaiming our vitality as a people means embracing a plant-based diet of whole foods. In our view, people can eat responsibly whether they are vegans, vegetarians, flexitarians, pescetarians, or omnivores. In a decolonial framework, there is room for multiple ways of eating, so we don't believe everyone needs to make the same food choices. We see the preparation of food as a creative act of resistance. While we are committed to reclaiming knowledge about our ancestral foods, including pre-contact food histories, we are not calling for a rejection of any food not native to the Americas, nor do we desire to recreate any one diet from a previous era. We understand that all cultures are living and evolving.

Decolonize Your Diet does not tout certain so-called "super foods"; instead, it is a whole food system of eating. Our *abuelitas* (grandmothers) prepared a simple diet that was as flavorful as it was nourishing. The staples of their diets were beans and tortillas, supplemented with many fruits and vegetables: avocados, corn, tomatoes, chiles, wild greens, squash, herbs, berries, pineapples, papayas, and more. They also had great knowledge of the medicinal value of their herbs and foods. So much of this knowledge is being lost, especially among those of us who have been in the US or away from the land

for generations. Many of our immigrant comrades—especially those who hail from rural areas in Mexico and Central America—still carry this vital knowledge. It is imperative that we validate and promote such knowledge and pass it down to future generations.

Anzaldúa ends her poem, "To survive in the Borderlands / you must live *sin fronteras* / be a crossroads." We share her advice to those of us who live in the borderlands, to retain our cultural identity, and to be "a crossroads"—a path for others to follow, a path toward health and strength. *Decolonize Your Diet* invites readers from diverse backgrounds to take up our call to bring playfulness and creativity to cooking, to search for healthy alternatives in more than one direction, to resist the acculturation that tells us white bread is food, and to share this message with your communities: *La comida es medicina*, food is medicine. We recognize that our book is only one step in this journey and that it provides only one small glimmer of the possibilities of a decolonized cuisine. We invite other chefs, writers, home cooks, bloggers, and activists to expand our project using the knowledge they collect from their own ancestors, regions, elders, communities, and ways of eating. We invite all our readers to use their creativity, taste, and historical memory to take our recipes and make them your own.

DECOLONIZE

◀ Ernesto Yerena Montejano, *Decolonize Maíz*, 2012, 18" x 24", silkscreen print. Reprinted courtesy of the artist

CHAPTER ONE

Decolonize!

Such food and drink my children, have made you sluggish and they make it difficult for you to reach the place of your ancestors. Those foods will bring you death. —from Historia de las Indias de Nueva España, *Fray Diego Durán, sixteenth century*

Allegory

The foods of the indigenous people of what is now Mexico and Central America have always been tied to stories about health and healing. We have found a story that was written down during the sixteenth century and probably circulated at least a hundred years earlier. It tells of pilgrims from the Aztec empire of Moctezuma I (c.1398–1469) sent by the emperor to seek out the original homeland of their people and to bring offerings to the goddess Coatlicue, mother of the main Aztec god Huitzilopochtli, the god of war. The pilgrims begin to climb the mountain to meet with the goddess, but with each step they sink into the sand. First they sink to their knees and then to their waists. They can no longer climb and are quickly left behind by their guide, an elder who walks lightly on the surface of the sand. This elder challenges them, "What is wrong with you, O Aztecs? What has made you so sluggish? What do you eat in your land?" When the pilgrims reply that they eat the rich foods and drink the valuable chocolate that the empire receives as tributes from the peoples they have conquered, the elder scolds them, telling them they have been weakened by their foods. "Here in the homeland," he says, "we know nothing of wealth and tribute, and yet our lives are much longer than yours and we are young and nimble." Leaving the pilgrims stuck in the sand, the elder carries their gifts up to

the mountain to offer them to Coatlicue. The goddess examines their gifts and also chastises them: "Is this food that you have brought me? This food is what burdens you. It weakens you and keeps you from climbing the hill." When she sends the pilgrims on their way, in place of the golden ornaments and feathered mantles that they have brought her, she gives them loin cloths and mantles made from coarse maguey fibers, and the simple food of the land, including the fish and birds of the lagoon, and many different kinds of plants.

This story is, at heart, a lesson about what it means to be people of the land. In the Aztec empire, the members of the ruling class are no longer subsistence farmers and hunters; instead they are warriors and oppressors who do not produce their food but extract it as tribute from the conquered peoples. The lesson of the pilgrims and the elder is that the food of empire, of stolen wealth, does not nourish the body or the soul. It does not sustain and it cannot be sustained. Almost 600 years later, this lesson is still relevant. The Standard American Diet cannot be sustained—its cost to the planet is too great—and it is literally making our people sick. In this book, we reclaim the indigenous foods that promote health; we embrace the idea of food as medicine. We believe that the simple foods of the land, which form the basis of indigenous heritage diets, have historically protected against and prevented the very diseases—diabetes, heart disease, high blood pressure, some cancers—that now threaten our communities' health.

Decolonize Your Diet: Food Is Medicine

Decolonization entails dismantling colonial systems of power and knowledge. Colonial systems take many forms; they structure and shape the economy, educational institutions, churches, and the food system. Economically, colonial powers extract wealth in the form of natural resources and labor to fund their enterprises, all the while taking land and resources away from indigenous communities. Within educational institutions in the Americas, colonial powers have set up hierarchies where European histories, ideas, and cultures are valued, while that which is indigenous is devalued, deprecated, and dismissed. The religious institutions of colonial powers relegate indigenous religions and spiritual practices to paganism and deviltry. Within Christianity, in particular, images of the divine are almost exclusively depicted as fair-skinned and with European features. *Decolonize Your Diet* challenges the ways in which European colonial powers characterize indigenous populations as being in need of education, religion, or culture. In our view, the opposite is true. The world needs to learn to listen to the teaching of indigenous peoples, and we need to recover the knowledge held by our indigenous ancestors.

In 1521, Spanish conquistadores, led by Hernán Cortés, conquered the city of Tenochtitlán, the capital and religious center of the *Mexica* (Aztec) empire. Over the ensuing centuries, millions of indigenous peoples were killed or died of diseases brought by the colonizers. Many indigenous people were forced to convert to Christianity. Some foods, such as amaranth in Mesoamerica and quinoa in the Andes, were outlawed because of their use in indigenous religious ceremonies. At the time of the Conquest, there were hundreds of indigenous groups, each with distinct languages, religious beliefs, and cultures. In the area that is now Mexico, in addition to the Mexica (Aztec) there were Mixtec, Zapotec, Maya, Purépecha, Otomi, Huichol, Tarahumara, Yaqui, Seri, O'odham, and many others. Over time, Spanish colonizers gained control of the land and resources of most of these indigenous groups, often through violent exertions of power. Because they were the most powerful group in Mesoamerica, there are many records about the Mexica culture at the time of the Conquest and, through study, we can learn quite a bit about their food, ceremonies, and social organization. Other indigenous groups keep this information through oral tradition, and it is not as widely known or recoverable to those of us not connected to our ancestors.

In the US, the Chicana/o movement of the 1960s and '70s argued that Chicana/o history and identity should be traced back to pre-Columbian civilizations, starting with the Olmecs (1500–400 BCE). This recovery of indigenous history and identity was disseminated in artwork, murals, poetry, literature, and Chicana/o Studies scholarship. The claim to indigenous ancestry was a counter-story to the then more popular construction of Mexican-Americans as having "Spanish" or "Latin" heritage. In recent decades, Chicana/o and Central American youth have carried this ethos forward, learning indigenous languages, such as Nahuatl; forming circles for ceremony, dance, and prayer; and participating in indigenous events across the continent.

We believe that indigenous cultural traditions in religion, art, music, literature, and food were never completely suppressed by the colonizers but kept alive, sometimes surreptitiously, through daily acts of storytelling, cooking, and prayer. In a Chicana/o context, one important site of this maintenance of indigenous knowledge and culture is the tradition of passing down recipes from generation to generation. Learning to make a corn tortilla or preparing a pot of tamales are practices that have been sustained for more than a thousand years. That we still engage in these practices today is a testament to our ancestors and their extraordinary knowledge about food.

Both of us have grandparents who spoke fondly of finding and preparing *quelites* (lamb's quarters) and

exist&
resist&
indigenize&
decolonize

verdolagas (purslane). *Quelites* comes from the Nahuatl word *quelitl*, meaning edible wild green. Technically, *verdolagas* are also a wild green and thus a subset of the larger group of *quelites*; however, in the US Southwest, our grandparents used the word *quelites* to refer specifically to lamb's quarters. *Verdolagas (Portulaca oleracea)* is often said to have originated in North Africa and the Middle East; however, there is considerable archeological evidence of its presence in the Americas before colonization. One type of lamb's quarters (*Chenopodium berlandieri*) is native to the Americas and is closely related to quinoa (*Chenopodium quinoa*). Another type of lamb's quarters is *Chenopodium album*, which is native to Europe and Asia. Throughout the world, agribusiness considers both *quelites* and *verdolagas* to be weeds and uses herbicides, such as Monsanto's Roundup, to try to kill these nutritious plants.

Global food activist Vandana Shiva critiques the single-minded corporate worldview that favors the eradication of biodiversity and modification of all nature into plantations for profit. She argues, "Not being commercially useful, people's crops [indigenous foods grown in indigenous ways] are treated as 'weeds' and destroyed with poisons. The most extreme example of this destruction is that of *bathua* (*Chenopodium album*), an important green leafy vegetable, with a very high nutritive value and rich in Vitamin A."[1] This *bathua*, regarded as a pernicious weed and a threat to commercial wheat crops, is the wild green our grandparents called *quelites*. Shiva brings attention to the horrific inhumanity of using weed killers on wild food crops: "Forty thousand children in India go blind each year for lack of Vitamin A, and herbicides contribute to this tragedy by destroying the freely available sources of Vitamin A [*bathua*]." According to Michael Pollan, "Two of the most nutritious plants in the world are weeds—lamb's quarters and purslane—and some of the healthiest traditional diets ... make frequent use of wild greens. The fields and forests are crowded with plants containing higher levels of various phytochemicals than their domesticated cousins."[2]

The Standard American Diet

When Michael Pollan advises in *Food Rules*, "Don't eat anything your grandmother wouldn't recognize," he's highlighting the ways in which the production of food in the early twenty-first century is wholly alienated not only from the way we live—we typically don't see where our food comes from—but from our

---

1 Vandana Shiva, "Monocultures of the Mind," in *The Vandana Shiva Reader* (Lexington, KY: The University Press of Kentucky, 2015), 84.

2 Michael Pollan, *In Defense of Food: An Eater's Manifesto* (New York: Penguin, 2008), 170.

own cultural histories and traditional food ways. The Standard American Diet relies heavily on highly processed foods and meat, poultry, and dairy produced on factory farms.

Real food has, for many of us and in many ways, become unrecognizable as such. Most Americans do not eat a plant-based diet with plenty of fresh fruits, vegetables, and herbs. Instead, North Americans consume a lot of sugary, fried, or fake foods like sodas, energy drinks, chips and other bagged snacks, candy bars, and cookies, which contain considerable amounts of high fructose corn syrup, sugar and artificial sweeteners, corn and soybean oils, and sodium. The average American eats 156 pounds (seventy-one kg) of added sugar every year. Not only are Americans eating these foods, they are eating more of them: per person we're now eating 750 more calories per day than we consumed thirty years ago. There are multiple factors that influence the dismal eating habits of many Americans. These include lack of access to healthy, fresh foods, which is a particular problem in working-class communities of color; easy access to fast food and junk food; advertising campaigns for sodas, fast food, and junk food that target youth; and agricultural subsidies that make processed and fake foods cheap and accessible.

Unlike immigrant Latinas/os who grew up with ready access to fresh foods grown and produced on small, local farms, many US-born Latinas/os have never even tasted real food. One study on immigrant diets found that immigrant Latinas who bought fresh food from street markets in the US reported that the food in their home countries was tastier, fresher, and "more natural." For US Latina/o communities, the Standard American Diet has been imposed through Americanization programs, school lunch programs, targeted advertising campaigns, and national food policies. Our communities are now riddled with the diseases of development—diabetes, high blood pressure, heart disease, and some cancers.

While we believe that individuals, families, and communities can take concrete steps to decolonize their diets by reintroducing traditional and ancestral foods, we recognize that a true solution to this problem will entail radical structural changes to the way food is produced, distributed, and consumed both in the US and globally. As we join others in calling for an end to the Standard American Diet of over-processed foods, we also want to challenge language that frames questions of health and diet as problems related only to an individual's "choices." This focus on the individual is especially pronounced in popular discussions of obesity. Although obesity is classified as a risk factor for diabetes, heart disease, and some cancers, the relationship between weight and disease is quite complex. It is important to keep in mind that there are healthy and

unhealthy people in all weight categories: underweight, "normal" weight, and overweight. We think the public focus on obesity makes it too easy to demonize individual fat people without seriously engaging with the social policies that are corrupting our food supply and, in turn, our health. A cultural obsession with being thin does not help our understanding of what it means to be healthy.

The Latina/o Immigrant Paradox

Public health scholars studying recent immigrants to the United States from Mexico and Central America have found that they have lower rates of infant mortality, overall mortality, and many illnesses, including certain cancers, compared to other population groups. (Overall mortality rates indicate the number of deaths per thousand people.) Hundreds of peer-reviewed scientific articles have been published describing this phenomenon that researchers call the "Latina/o Immigrant Paradox." Researchers have not found a definitive explanation for this paradox.

We believe that immigrant good health can be attributed, at least in part, to the fact that many immigrants were raised on a diet of ancestral foods. The superior health of the Mexican and Central American immigrant community is impressive, given that these immigrants face so many challenges. Most often, they arrive with very few economic resources; they don't have access to preventative health care and are often afraid to seek care when they are sick; they face racism, economic exploitation, and uncertain futures for their families; they work in difficult and dangerous jobs; they live in economically disenfranchised communities; and, for all these reasons, they live with extremely high levels of social, spiritual, and economic stress. Ordinarily, given the class and social status of most immigrants, public health researchers would expect them to have the very worst health outcomes. That they have some of the best health outcomes is the reason this is called a paradox.

Several studies on immigrant women from Mexico and Central America have found that they have healthier babies and fewer pregnancy and birth complications when compared to other communities of color and when compared to average Americans. The rates of infant mortality and low birth weight for Mexican immigrant mothers have remained low for decades. At a 2003 conference on Mexican immigration in New York City, surgeon Carlos Navarro noted that "Mexican immigrant women have healthy babies. They have some sort of cultural advantage, but we [doctors] don't know what it is."[3]

---

3 Alyshia Gálvez, *Patient Citizens, Immigrant Mothers: Mexican Women, Public Prenatal Care, and the Birth-weight Paradox* (New Brunswick, NJ: Rutgers University Press, 2011), 2.

◀ Veronica Perez, *Seeds of Resistance*, 2010, acrylic on canvas, 20" x 24". Reprinted courtesy of the artist

A study of low breast cancer rates among Latinas in the US shows that Latina/o diets are high in fiber, which may protect against breast cancer because it modulates estrogen levels. The Latinas studied were found to have higher than average fiber intake, mostly from fruits, vegetables, corn tortillas, grains, and beans in their diets.

Unfortunately, studies done on Latina/o immigrant health in the US have also shown that the health of immigrants declines the longer they stay in the US and the more they assimilate into US culture. By the second generation, US-born Latinas/os face similar issues as other communities of color in the US, with skyrocketing rates of diabetes and cardiovascular disease. Rates of certain lifestyle-related cancers also start to increase. The 2005 study of Latinas show higher breast cancer rates among Latinas who were second-generation, English speaking, and/or of higher income levels.

In addition to the health benefit being lost by US-born Latinas/os, healthy indigenous traditions are also at risk throughout Mexico and Central America. The situation for Mexico's rural and indigenous poor is quickly changing. NAFTA (the North American Free Trade Agreement signed in 1994) has disrupted traditional land use in Mexico's rural areas. Indigenous farmers, in particular, are being forced off their land and are now among the groups most likely to leave Mexico for the US and Canada. Those who stay in rural Mexican communities are beginning to rely on ever-increasing amounts of processed commodity food, much of it imported from the US. The traditional corn tortilla is now in danger of contamination from GMOs, as they are sometimes produced with US-grown GM corn, even in Mexico. While this situation is dire, there are also hopeful signs. In Mexico, food sovereignty movements have become important sites of resistance. Composed of peasant and indigenous organizations, the coalition *Red en Defensa del Maíz* has articulated the urgent need to reject GM corn. As a result of activism from this and many other groups, in 2013, Federal Court District Judge Jaime Eduardo Verdugo of Mexico City wrote that the GM corn posed "the risk of imminent harm to the environment" and instituted an immediate ban on GM corn seed everywhere in Mexico. Organizing continues to assure that the ban stays in place and also extends the ban to the importing of GM corn and corn products.

> *The planting of transgenic maize [GMO corn] is a frontal attack against native and peasant peoples and a violation of their rights. For the peoples that constitute Mexico, maize is not merchandise, but the origin of a civilization and the foundation of peasant lives and economies. We will not let our seeds be lost or contaminated by transgenes [GMOs] owned by transnational companies. We will not comply with unfair laws that criminalize seeds and peasant life ways. We will continue protecting maize and the life of our peoples.*" —Red en Defensa del Maíz[4]

Reclaiming Native Foods

Before contact with Europeans, native peoples in what is now Mexico, Central America, and the US Southwest ate many foods unknown to Europeans. At the time of Conquest, the lifespan of the Aztecs exceeded that of the Spaniards by ten years.[5] The Aztecs were purported to describe the Spaniards' food as "sick people's food," contrasting it to their own cuisine, which included an array of delicious fruits, vegetables, sauces, and meats prepared with a wide variety of cooking techniques. Foods indigenous to the Americas (e.g., tomatoes, potatoes) have, in the past 500 years, changed the diet of the planet. However, Mexican and Central American cuisine also changed. The Spanish colonizers introduced white flour, cane sugar, and beef, among other products. They also introduced new methods of cook-ing, such as frying. After colonization, the grain base in the Americas has shifted from a reliance on corn and amaranth to predominantly wheat and rice.

Historical descriptions of the food markets in Tlatelolco (near modern-day Mexico City) speak to a plethora of foods and culinary techniques. In 1520, Hernán Cortés describes his first impression of the city market in a letter written to Charles V of Spain. He estimated that there were more than 60,000 people in the daily market, twice the size of its contemporary in Salamanca, Spain. Each section of the market featured an entire street devoted to a particular kind of food. The meat vendors sold fifteen kinds of game birds, as well as rabbits and venison. The description of fruits and vegetables is also impressive:

> There are all sorts of vegetables, and espe-cially onions, leeks, garlic, borage, nasturtium, water-cresses, sorrel, thistles, and artichokes.

4 A. Richard, "Sin Maíz No Hay Pais: Citizenship and Environment in Mexico's Food Sovereignty Movement," in *Environment and Citizenship in Latin America*. Hannah Wittman and Alex Latta, eds. (Amsterdam: Centre for Latin American Research and Documentation (CEDLA)/Berghahn Books, 2012).

5 Anne-Emanuelle Birn, "Public Health and Medicine in Latin America," in *The Oxford Handbook of the History of Medicine*, Mark Jackson, ed. (Oxford: Oxford University Press, 2011), 243–265.

Florentine Codex, volume 10, chapter 19, no. 127. "Tamale Vendor"

There are many kinds of fruits, amongst others cherries, and prunes, like the Spanish ones. They sell bees-honey and wax, and honey made from corn stalks … also honey of a plant called maguey … They sell maize, both in the grain and made into bread, which is very superior in its quality to that of the other islands and mainland; pies of birds, and fish, also much fish, fresh, salted, cooked, and raw; eggs of hens, and geese, and other birds in great quantity, and cakes made of eggs.[6]

From this description, we see a glimpse of the incredible biodiversity available in pre-Conquest times. As we looked at the list of foods that Cortés encountered at the market, we were surprised to see onions, garlic, plums, and cherries listed, for those are commonly thought to have originated outside the Americas. However, research reveals that wild onions (*Allium drummondii*), wild garlic (*Allium canadense*), plums (*Prunus americana*), and cherries (*Eugenia uniflora*) were all confirmed in the Americas before the Conquest.

The original inhabitants of the Americas cultivated and harvested a staggering variety of plant-based foods. The four food staples of ancient Mexico were corn, beans, amaranth, and chia, which provided abundant bioavailable protein. Moreover, it is important to note that extensive trade routes existed before colonization, with indigenous people from diverse cultures and locations involved in exchanges of food, seeds, and cooking utensils, not only in the Tlatelolco marketplace but throughout the hemisphere.

While there is much to learn from our *abuelitas*' (grandmothers') kitchens, where food was home cooked and often home grown, we want to look to even earlier generations, before white flour, sugar, and milk entered into the picture. Most people fluent in Mexican cuisine believe that a traditional red chile sauce begins with a roux made of white flour and vegetable oil or lard, but it wasn't always prepared that way. In Pre-Conquest Mexico, people used chia or pumpkin seeds or corn *masa* (dough) to thicken sauces. When Spanish explorers returned to Europe with corn, it was regarded only as a grain to be prepared and used like wheat, rice, or barley. Corn became a staple in Italy, where it was peasant food. When the poor Italian peasants ate it as a staple, they developed pellagra, a disease cause by lack of niacin in the diet. Native peoples, however, knew that when corn is hulled and treated with wood ash or slaked lime (a process called nixtamalization), it is more nourishing; the process unlocks the niacin, making it bio-available.

6 Hernán Cortés, *Fernando Cortes: His Five Letters of Relation to the Emperor Charles V*, translated by Francis Augustus McNutt (Cleveland, OH: A. H. Clark, 1908), 257–59.

Codex Mendoza: Girl Making Tortillas

The Florentine Codex, a 2,400-page document (in twelve volumes), details many aspects of Mexica (Aztec) food, agriculture, and ceremony as practiced at the time of the Conquest. The *Codex* was written in Nahuatl and Spanish by Mexica scribes and informants under the direction of Franciscan missionary Bernardino de Sahagún (1499–1590). The purpose of the *Codex* was to document all aspects of Mexica culture in great detail. We are especially drawn to the elaborate descriptions of the *tamalli* vendor in Volume Ten. The good *tamalli* vendor is described as selling tamales of various shapes and sizes, with a wide array of fillings: some round, some tied, some folded; some wrapped in corn husks, some in banana leaves; some with sweet, fruit-studded *masa*, some with savory spiced *masa* or tangy, fermented *masa*; some stuffed with turkey, beans, seeds, fish or other meats; some baked and some steamed. There were dozens, perhaps hundreds, of ways to make tamales. They describe sweet fillings including fruit, honey, and beeswax. The savory tamales include chile—"they burn within!"—or tomatoes, pumpkin seeds, pumpkin, or squash blossoms. Good tamales are described in enticing language: "very tasty, very well made … savory … of very pleasing odor … Where [it is] tasty [it has] chile, salt, tomatoes, gourd seeds: shredded, crumbled, juiced." The long, detailed description of the tamales in the pre-Columbian era fills us with awe and wonder, but it should be noted that the *Florentine Codex* also delineates the person who sells "bad" tamales: "The bad food seller is one who sells filthy tamales, discolored tamales—broken, tasteless, quite tasteless, inedible, frightening, deceiving … [tamales]."

Like all cooks, when we cook with each other's families, with our friends, and with cookbooks, we come across the inevitable argument about the "right" way to cook a dish, with each side arguing that theirs is the "authentic" version. These arguments might be based on regional preferences, such as how to wrap tamales: Folded or tied? Wrapped in corn husks or banana leaves? Or the argument could be about a preferred ingredient: Lard or shortening? Meat or pumpkin? By reading the codices, we've learned that indigenous peoples of Mesoamerica have always made many different kinds of tamales, and this encourages us to be creative and bold, instead of imagining that there is one "authentic" recipe that we need to emulate. Generation after generation, our ancestors fed their families and communities by being clever, adaptable, and ingenious, and by making use of different available ingredients.

Liberate the Kitchen

For many Mexican and Central American women, cooking is something they have been forced to do, part of the construction of womanhood, something to which they may submit or resist or which they may resent. Since the 1970s, for many Chicanas the image of

Florentine Codex, Patlache

I've realized that Luz is like the *tamalli* vendor in
   the codices:
They make tamales with jack cheese and green
   chile *nuevomexicano* and sweet corn;
with goat cheese, lemon zest, and black olives;
with butternut squash, *rajas*, and *queso Oaxaca*;

They make vegan tamales, with chipotle and
   potato;
with green chile and pumpkin;
with *hongos creminis*, maitakes, shiitake, oyster;

They make sweet tamales with blackberries;
with chocolate—they warm, they incite!;
with dried *piña* and cranberries;
with sweet beans and sweet spices …

Their masa is organic,
is hand-ground,
uses white corn,
uses blue corn,
has sweet corn kernels,
has chia seeds,
has herb leaves,
is flavored with broth,
is flavored with oolong tea,
is flavored with *jamaica*,
is flavored with flowers of *yerbanís*.

They serve their tamales with sauces;
with blackberry sauce for sweet tamales;
with fig jam for goat cheese tamales;
with *chile colorado* for savory tamales.

The bad tamale maker forgets to salt the masa;
over-salts the masa;
spreads the masa too thick, they are *masudos*;
overcooks the tamales, they are dry, their skin is
   rubbery;
forgets the steamer on the stove and the pot
   boils dry, the *hojas* are burned.

> *As descendants of Mexican and Central American immigrants, many of us know very little about our indigenous ancestors. Many of us don't have a single community or indigenous group to claim. Some of us participate in ceremonies that rekindle those lost connections. For example, Mexica (Aztec) dance continues to the present day, kept alive in social/spiritual groups called calpullis, which take their name from a Nahuatl word originally meaning villages, pueblos, or barrios (neighborhoods). All over North America today, calpullis meet weekly or monthly, teaching and performing traditional dances. There is a dance to Tlaloc, the Rain God, to Tonantzin, the Earth Goddess, and to Maíz, which acts out the many steps to planting and harvesting corn.*

the Mexican mother making tortillas was held in direct contrast to that of the liberated Chicana daughter who earned her own money and set her own terms. The problem is that sometimes, in our haste to liberate ourselves from the kitchen, we ended up devaluing the work that our mothers and grandmothers performed. Our liberation from the kitchen meant that we lost touch with how our foods formed an intrinsic part of our cultural heritage and our health. Likewise, for every story of an angry young Chicana who resisted and resented learning to cook, there is a story of a young Chicano shamed for wanting to spend time in the kitchen, warned to walk away from women's work, and challenged about his masculinity and his sexuality.

We believe that any activity that is forced or coerced becomes oppressive. We understand that under conditions of patriarchy, food preparation often becomes an unpleasant task. In the mid-twentieth century, advertising and the food industry promised quick fixes such as frozen or processed foods or prepackaged meals that could feed everyone cheaply and quickly. Family cooks were told not to "waste time," and the work of preparing food was not acknowledged as essential to survival and building community. Fast food seems like liberation from the sexual politics of food preparation, but this so-called solution is having disastrous consequences. We are, in effect, giving up control of our sustenance to an industry whose primary concern will always be to turn a profit. Fast food is toxic to our people, our animal relatives, and Mother Earth. We need to find another way.

We believe that any cookbook and discussion of food preparation that doesn't address the gendered conditions of labor may be seen to reinforce oppressive relations. We are *not* calling for a return of Chicanas and Central American women to the kitchen. We are calling for the liberation *of* the kitchen. We understand that food is one of the pillars of our survival as a people. We need to find ways to truly value the labor that goes into all aspects of food preparation: growing, gathering, raising, distributing, and cooking food as well as the labor of keeping the kitchen clean and well-stocked.

In every household, communal living space, or *calpulli*, the division of labor needs to be open to discussion and negotiation. In concrete terms, this means identifying the different kinds of work essential to feeding the group—gardening, meal planning, shopping, cooking, or cleanup—and dividing these tasks in ways that are equitable. The ultimate goal should be to reconfigure the tasks themselves so that, as much as possible, the activities of procuring and preparing food can be experienced as a playful, spiritual, creative practice by everyone. In short, we want to rework the activities of the kitchen so that they become central to the revolutionary practice of love.

We welcome the fact that most people now recognize that families are configured in many ways and that families can be units of people related by blood, as well as units that come together by choice. Similarly, the labor within families can also be organized in many ways. There is no one right way to be a family, and there is no one right way to divide the tasks that go into cooking fresh, healthy meals. As queer Chicanas/os, we recognize that the kitchen has been a space to which many women have been confined, yet also one in which many (men, women, and two-spirit) have laid their own claim. Activist meetings should include feeding each other healthy foods. If one person prepares a pan of enchiladas, another a pot of beans, another a nopales salad, and another a pitcher of hibiscus tea, then the whole group is strengthened, nourished, and sustained.

Indigenous Action for Food Sovereignty

As more Chicanas/os and Central Americans come to recognize our indigenous heritages, we support and draw from the struggles of contemporary Native peoples. Our project is influenced by American Indian and First Nation scholars, activists, and chefs who are challenging the devastation wrought on indigenous communities by the Standard American Diet. Winona LaDuke (Anishinaabe) writes that, "Indigenous communities have survived an incredible set of ordeals related to food, nutrition, medicine and life, and continue to keep their cultural traditions alive. They also continue to plant seeds passed from ancestors a thousand years ago so that they can eventually pass them on to their grandchildren."[7]

We cannot overemphasize the importance of seeds: like recipes, they are a cultural inheritance passed down from generation to generation. At this point in history, we see an urgent need to resist GM seeds and to support the struggle against GMOs in Mexico and Central America, where people have been organizing against GM corn, in particular. Agribusiness focuses on monoculture, raising one crop in huge fields and applying pesticides and herbicides. In contrast, indigenous ways of cultivation use intercropping, which grows more than

7 Winona LaDuke with Sarah Alexander, *Food Is Medicine: Recovering Traditional Foods to Heal the People* (Honor the Earth, Minneapolis, MN: Honor the Earth, 2004), 34.

COLONIZED DIET	DECOLONIZED DIET
White Supremacy and Americanization programs	respect for indigenous knowledge, cultural revitalization
disavowal, thoughtlessness	intentions, blessings, and gratitude
refined foods: white sugar, white flour, high fructose corn syrup	whole foods: nixtamalized corn, whole grains, mesquite, local honey
wasteful	resourceful
advertising, marketing, and fads	ancestral knowledge, oral tradition
pesticides and monoculture	permaculture, intercropping, organically grown
GMO seeds	heritage seeds, seed saving
NAFTA, agribusiness	small farms, local control, truly fair trade
food for profit	food to sustain life
assimilation	resistance, resilience

one crop in the same field. One well-known example of intercropping is the "Three Sisters" technique, where corn, squash, and beans are grown together. Among the many benefits of this technique is that the beans "fix" nitrogen in the soil, which helps the corn grow tall and strong without the need for chemical fertilizers.

We are indebted to Devon Abbott Mihesuah (Choctaw), who makes the argument that, "One symptom of accepting colonization is adhering to the typical American Diet, even while it is killing us."[8] Her words summarize our entire project: we must reject colonization because this diet is literally killing us. Mihesuah makes clear that diseases such as diabetes are the legacy of a 500-year effort to eradicate indigenous peoples. She points out the contradictions in dietary guidelines that promote dairy products despite widespread lactose intolerance among Native peoples and in spite of the fact that dietary calcium is readily available from dark leafy greens. Upon exploring how US government policies have destroyed the agriculture and radically changed the diet of American Indians, Mihesuah issues a rallying cry to Native peoples: "Eating the foods this society presents without questioning the contents of those dishes and the damaging or healthful benefits of those foods is one of the manifestations [of coloniza-

tion]. One huge step we can take to regain our culture and pride is to grow, cultivate, and prepare our own foods that our ancestors ate."[9] Mihesuah connects her knowledge of and research on Choctaw culture to a plan for reclaiming traditional foods and emphasizing traditional forms of physical exercise like gardening, running, stickball, and walking.

Our project has also been deeply inspired by the Tohono O'odham in Arizona, an American Indian nation whose members have been active in reclaiming native foods as a way of restoring health. The Tohono O'odham, who have one of the highest rates of diabetes in the world, worked with Native Seeds/SEARCH co-founder Gary Nabhan in a study that reconstructed a nineteenth-century O'odham diet and examined its effects on the people. After two weeks on a diet of traditional foods high in fiber and complex carbohydrates and low in fats, the participants saw significant improvement in their blood sugar levels. They then spent two weeks on a Standard American Diet based on foods available in a local convenience store. During the second two weeks, the participants showed dramatically higher blood sugar levels, "severe enough to trigger diabetes if that diet had been maintained." The activist group Tohono O'odham Community Action

---

8 Devon A. Mihesuah, "Decolonizing Our Diets By Recovering Our Ancestors' Gardens," *American Indian Quarterly* 27, no. 3/4 (Summer–Autumn 2003), 827.

9 Devon Abbot Mihesuah, *Recovering Our Ancestor's Gardens: Indigenous Recipes and Guide to Diet and Fitness* (Lincoln, NB: University of Nebraska Press, 2005), 58.

Talk to elders in your community about the foods they ate growing up: What foods did they eat then that are no longer available? How was food prepared? What herbs and plants did they use for medicine? How did they conduct their ceremonies?

(TOCA) has a self-published book, *From I'itoi's Garden: Tohono O'odham Food Traditions* (2010) that is a beautiful cultural resource featuring history; traditional stories; growing, foraging, and harvesting techniques; songs; and recipes. The authors focus on ten native foods of the Sonoran desert: squash, acorns, cholla buds, saguaro cactus, mesquite pods, prickly pear fruit, agave, wild greens, sixty-day corn, and tepary beans, plus other domesticated and wild foods. Through actively reclaiming their heritage foods, the Tohono O'odham are fighting the diseases inflicted on their people by the Standard American Diet.

These examples of direct action by indigenous groups demonstrate clearly the ways in which personal food choices are also political acts. We honor our ancestors and their wisdom by learning how to cook beans, make corn tortillas from scratch, and forage for and grow wild foods like *quelites*. By sharing our knowledge with each other and by becoming active in our communities, we can begin to decolonize our diets.

Our Decolonial Kitchen

Our recipes feature farm fresh fruits and vegetables, dried beans, fresh herbs, spices, and whole flours made from native grains like amaranth, corn, and quinoa. To us, "farm fresh" means ingredients that come from our backyard garden, farmer's markets, or the produce section. We shop at the local Mexican market, Asian markets, health food stores, and grocery stores that sell organic produce. We occasionally buy some specialty items online. We embrace a made-from-scratch approach to cooking, and our recipes range from very simple to more complex. The great majority of ingredients in our recipes are native to the Americas. We cook with native vegetables such as green chiles, nopales, tomatoes, squash, corn, chayotes, and green beans. Native fruits we feature include berries, currants, avocados, papayas, passion fruit, pineapples, and prickly pears. We are big fans of foraged greens, such as *verdolagas, quelites*, and watercress, and we incorporate them into many of our recipes.

Most cookbooks highlight Mesoamerican food as a productive encounter between indigenous and Spanish ingredients, producing a splendid hybrid cuisine. Our recipes take another path, focusing on the indigenous history that is embedded in contemporary Mexican and Central American cuisine. We try to recreate dishes as they might have existed before the Conquest, before wheat flour, sugar, beef, dairy, or cooking oils. That said, we are not purists. Our overriding concern is to create dishes that nourish the body and the spirit. We include small amounts of cheese and a bit of oil when we feel that those ingredients help to balance or develop flavors. All of our recipes are vegetarian, with many providing vegan options. Likewise, because there was no wheat flour before colonization, most of our recipes are also gluten-free. We go back to the old ways and thicken our sauces, stews, and soups with masa harina (corn flour) or ground pumpkin seeds, instead of white flour. All of our recipes feature whole, real foods that are unrefined and unprocessed, or in the case of flours, made from whole grains.

We envision these recipes as living documents that you can change and revise to meet the needs of your friends and family. Don't be afraid to substitute based on what you have on hand or what is readily available. Our recipes sometimes call for seasonal fruits or vegetables that may not be available in all areas. We offer substitutions as a short-term solution, but we hope that by introducing you to using beautiful ingredients like local green chiles, *quelites*, or *verdolagas*, we will entice you to grow them yourselves or inquire about them at your local farmer's market. We hope more people will take up this project and share and publish recipes that recover foods from their own regions and backgrounds.

Finally, the most important ingredient for our recipes is not listed anywhere. This secret ingredient is the love that you put into preparing your food. Whether you are the cook, the gardener, or part of the clean-up crew, please know that your labor is sacred and that somewhere the ancestors are smiling, knowing that you are taking an active role in healing your friends and family from the ravages of the ¡Qué SAD! diet.

CHAPTER TWO
Our Mesoamerican Pantry

In this section, we share the ingredients, tools, and techniques that have become part of our everyday practice of cooking healthy Mesoamerican-inspired meals. For ingredients, we provide historical notes, purchasing suggestions, and information for substitutions, where possible. There are a few basic kitchen tools that we have come to rely upon. The cooking techniques are basic and we provide step-by-step directions.

Ingredients ....

Achiote (also called annatto)

The seeds of the achiote tree are sold as seeds, powder, or paste. They are extremely hard and when infused in oil, turn it a luscious orange-red color. The powder is useful for adding directly to soups and stews. This spice dates back to pre-Conquest Mexico, where it was also used in cacao drinks. Its flavor is described as earthy or woodsy. Achiote paste often has preservatives and artificial colors, so we prefer to use seeds or powder.

Allspice berries

The dried berries of this evergreen shrub, native to Southern Mexico, Central America, and the Greater Antilles, have a rich spicy scent and flavor. It has been described as a combination of the all the spices (clove, ginger, cinnamon, nutmeg, and pepper).

Amaranth (seeds, flour, and leaves)

Often called an ancient "grain," amaranth is actually a seed. It is sold whole or as flour. Generally available in health food stores, it's also found in the bulk section and sold as Rajgira in South Asian markets. It is also widely available to purchase online (see Sources, p. 239). If you grow the plant (it's lovely!), the tender leaves are delicious additions to salads and can be cooked like spinach or *quelites* (see p. 47). Amaranth greens are sometimes available at farmer's markets.

Avocado leaves

You can find dried leaves of the Mexican avocado (*P. americana* var. *drymifolia*) in the spice section of your local Mexican market or online (see Sources, p. 239). Avocado leaves impart a delicate anise flavor to bean dishes. *Note*: Only use leaves from a Mexican avocado; the leaves of the Guatemalan avocado (*Persea nubigena* var. *guatamalensis*) are thought to be toxic. Do not cook with leaves from your own avocado tree unless you are absolutely certain it is a non-toxic variety.

Beans, dried

The original inhabitants of the Americas had four main domesticated beans: the tepary bean (*Phaseolus acutifolius*), the scarlet runner bean (*Phaseolus coccineus*), the lima bean (*Phaseolus lunatus*), and the common bean (*Phaseolus vulgaris*). Most of the beans we cook with are in the class of common beans, which includes black, red, yellow, white, striped, and speckled beans, such as pinto, Anasazi, and cranberry beans. In the past, indigenous peoples cultivated thousands of different varieties of the common bean, specific to different locales, microclimates, and altitudes. Regular consumption of beans has been shown to lower cholesterol and high blood pressure and to normalize blood sugar.

Tepary beans come in many colors, each with their own unique flavor. They have a lower glycemic index and higher level of protein than most other beans. They are being recovered from extinction by the Tohono O'odham people in Arizona and can be bought online (see Sources, p. 239). Allow slightly more time to cook than other dried beans.

Butter, pastured

Although butter is not a pre-Conquest food, we do occasionally use real butter in our recipes. We recommend "pastured" butter, that is, butter from cows who eat real grass, because the bodies of ruminants evolved specifically to digest grasses. Conventional butter is from cows that are fed corn and soy, often genetically modified, and usually in Concentrated Animal Feeding Operations, which provide unhealthy conditions for the cattle and pollute the land and water with waste products. Pastured butter is an excellent source of conjugated linoleic acid (CLA), which is thought to have important cancer-fighting properties.

Cacao, raw (ground)

Raw ground cacao is a great way to get the full health benefits of cacao without additives or sweeteners. We use it in our chocolate desserts. You can buy this in the raw food section of health food stores, and it is also widely available online (see Sources, p. 239).

Cashews

Although we think of cashews as nuts, they grow at the bottom of a native fruit, the cashew apple. Blended with water, cashews make a good vegan substitute for Mexican *crema* (a thin sour cream).

Chaya (*Cnidoscolus aconitifolius*)

Also known as "tree spinach," chaya is a tropical plant from the Veracruz region of Mexico. It is often used as a treatment for diabetes. Fresh chaya is not sold commercially in the United States, but dried chaya is sold as a medicinal tea. Several online vendors sell living plants. If you want to grow one yourself, know that it needs a warm climate or should be kept indoors.

Chayote (*Sechium edule*)

This green vegetable grows on a vine, and some varieties have spines. The flesh is white and can be eaten raw or cooked. It is available at ethnic markets and is easy to grow, but not from seed. The chayote fruit itself will sprout, and once it does, can be planted in the ground. It will die back during winter but return in the spring. Chayote needs room to grow and can easily cover a trellis, fence, or roof.

Chia (*Salvia hispanica*)

This small ancient seed, used by native runners to fuel long journeys, is nutrient dense. It is used in drinks,

to thicken stews, or in baked goods, and is widely available in health food stores.

Chiles, dried

Dried chiles add flavor, heat, and color to sauces and salsas. Varieties include guajillo, pasilla, ancho, chipotle, and chiltepines (the wild "grandmother" of chiles). These are widely available in Mexican and Central American markets and online (see Sources, p. 239). Organic dried chiles are more difficult to source, but are sometimes available at farmers markets. Eating plenty of dried chiles has cardiovascular benefits, boosts immunity, and lowers risk for type 2 diabetes.

Chiles, fresh

Larger green chiles, such as New Mexico Green, Anaheim, or poblanos, are roasted and peeled. These can be stuffed (chiles rellenos) or torn into strips (*rajas*) to add a delicious roasted flavor and (usually) mild heat to dishes. These large chiles can be used interchangeably based on what is available. The smaller chiles, such as the jalapeño and serrano, which tend to be hotter, can be used either raw or cooked in dishes and salsas. Taste chiles before adding them to dishes to determine the level of heat you desire.

Chipotle en adobo

Commonly sold in cans, the chipotle is a smoked, dried jalapeño preserved in sauce. We provide a recipe (p. 167) to make this from scratch, but the canned version is widely available and can be used as a substitute.

Cinnamon

Cinnamon is not a native spice but has become a key ingredient in Mexican cuisine. Among its many health benefits, it is especially good for balancing blood sugar levels. We include cinnamon in our recipes because diabetes has become such a concern in our communities. We recommend using Ceylon cinnamon (also called *canela Mexicana*), which has a less astringent flavor profile than the more common *Cinnamomum cassia*. However, both types have medicinal properties, so feel free to substitute *cassia* if Ceylon cinnamon is not available. When buying whole cinnamon sticks, it is easy to distinguish between the two: Ceylon cinnamon will easily break apart in your hand, while *cassia* is virtually unbreakable.

Corn, fresh and frozen

Our recipes call for fresh corn kernels. One ear of corn will yield between ¾ and 1 cup (175–250 mL) kernels. In winter months, frozen corn is an adequate substitution. We recommend buying organic corn, since most conventionally grown corn in the US is from genetically modified seeds.

Corn husks

Dried corn husks are sold in Mexican markets. Soak them in warm water to make them soft and pliable, so they can be used to wrap tamales.

Epazote (*Dysphania ambrosioides*)

An herb native to Mexico, Central and South America, its Nahuatl name is *epazotl*. Used to flavor beans and sauces, it is also used medicinally, in small amounts, to treat intestinal disturbances and worms in humans and animals. It is best when used fresh, and is also available dried in the spice section of Mexican and Central American markets.

Hibiscus flowers (jamaica)

Dried hibiscus flowers, called Jamaica, are sold in Mexican markets and in some herb stores, both brick-and-mortar and online. These flowers are high in vitamin C and make a tasty drink. We also use them as a filling for tacos (p. 133).

Hominy, dried or canned

Hominy is corn that has been treated with slaked lime, also called cal, and is sold either dried or canned. Untreated dried corn is not an adequate substitute, as it will not cook properly. However, it is possible to treat the dried corn with slaked lime. See p. 58 (Making Nixtamal).

Honey, raw local

Our recipes use raw local honey in small amounts. Raw local honey brings its own health benefits and is thought to help with allergy symptoms. Find truly local honey at farmer's markets and health food stores. Avoid "table syrup," sold in many markets, as it is a combination of honey, high fructose corn syrup, and/or sucrose.

Jícama

An edible tuberous root, its Nahuatl name is *xicamatl*. Jícama has a thin, brown skin that must be peeled before it can be eaten. The inside has a crisp texture, like a pear, which makes it a lovely addition to salads. Jícama is mostly water, but contains oligofructose inulin, a prebiotic that is beneficial to health.

Maple syrup, pure

Maple syrup is a sweetener native to the Americas. Use only products labeled as 100 percent (or "pure") maple syrup. Beware of "maple-flavored pancake syrup," which is full of high-fructose corn syrup.

Masa, fresh

A *tortillería* (a store where tortillas are made and sold) will sell fresh masa, made from nixtamalized corn. This masa is ground fresh each day and comes in a couple of varieties. *Masa para tortillas* (for tortillas) is a fine grind, used to make corn tortillas, with nothing added—it's

just corn and slaked lime, also called cal, used to nix-tamalize the corn. *Masa para tamales* (for tamales) is a coarser grind that's used for making tamales. Masa *para tamales* comes in two forms. The first is *preparada* (prepared), which means that some kind of shorten-ing (lard or vegetable) and salt has been added. The second form is *sin preparar* (wthout added salt or shortening). We always ask for *sin preparar* so that we can choose the quality and quantity of shortening use. Unfortunately, most *tortillerías* use conventionally grown (GM) corn, although some do have access to GMO-free or organic corn.

Masa harina (also called nixtamalized corn flour)
Corn that has been treated with slaked lime (cal), and then dried and ground into flour. It is rehydrated with water to make masa that can be used for tama-les, tortillas, and tlacoyos. Organic, GMO-free masa harina is available for purchase (see Sources, p. 239). *Note*: Corn flour or corn meal are not acceptable substitutions.

Mesquite flour
When people think of mesquite, they often think of smoky flavoring: For barbecues, chips of mesquite wood are soaked in water and then added to the fire to bring out the smoke and flavor meats. Mesquite trees produce long pods. The Tohono O'odham and other Native peoples of the Sonora and Chihuahua deserts gather and dry the pods and then grind them into flour. Mesquite flour adds an almost molasses-like flavor to dishes, and consumption can help regulate blood sugar.

Nopales
The nopal is the prickly pear cactus. The paddles of the cactus are a delicacy, but are also used for treating and preventing diabetes. The cactus produces fruit, and there are many varieties of prickly pear fruit: red, green, yellow, sweet, and sour. Both the paddles and the fruits are sold in the produce sections of Mexican markets. They are easy to grow in warm climates: simply plant a nopal paddle in the ground, and it will grow. You can also order the plant from online nurseries. If you can't find fresh nopales, look for jars in the canned goods section in Mexican grocery stores.

Oils
Before the Conquest, very little oil was used in cook-ing, but contemporary Mexican cuisine uses a lot of oil for frying. We have eliminated frying in many of our recipes, and we think the results are outstanding and even more delicious than the fried versions. We elim-inate oils not because we believe in a low-fat diet: we advocate eating healthy fats, especially from avocados. However, most vegetable oils used for cooking are

highly processed and are not healthy. When we sauté, we use small amounts of either extra virgin coconut oil or olive oil. Most of our dishes feature bold, spicy flavors that we find are a good foil to the coconut oil, which is safe to use at high heat. For finishing and dressings, we use extra virgin olive oil, pumpkin seed oil, or avocado oil.

Oregano, Mexican

The most common Mexican oregano is *Lippia graveolens*, a flowering plant in the verbena family. This plant is native to the US Southwest, Mexico, and Central America. The plant is sometimes called *orégano Cimmaron* or *hierba dulce*. *Lippia graveolens* contains thymol, carvacrol, para-cymene, and eucalyptol, which are potent anti-cancer phytochemicals. The first two components give the plant a flavor similar to oregano. The leaves are widely used as an herb in Mexican and Central American cuisine. Another herb, *Poliomintha longiflora*, is also sometimes called Mexican oregano. This is an entirely different plant that has exceptionally high levels of antioxidants. We grow both plants in our garden. You can find dried Mexican oregano online (see Sources, p. 239) and at many Mexican markets. Italian or Greek oregano (*Origanum vulgare*) are acceptable substitutes and also provide many health benefits.

Piloncillo

An unrefined, minimally processed form of sugar cane, *piloncillo* contains many minerals that are essential for health, unlike white sugar. *Piloncillo* is pressed into cones, which are sold at Mexican markets. Because the cones come in different sizes and are not standardized, we also provide measurement in ounces and grams. If you cannot find *piloncillo*, substitute jaggery or muscovado sugar.

Pumpkin seeds (*pepitas*)

In ancient times, pumpkins were grown mostly for their seeds, which are nutritious—high in protein and in healthy fats. We use them in salads, to thicken and flavor sauces, and in desserts and snacks. Buy raw, hulled seeds and then toast them in a frying pan. You'll know when they are done because they will puff up.

Quelites

From the Nahuatl word *quilitl* which means simply "wild greens." While *quelites* is sometimes used to describe all edible wild greens, we use it to refer specifically to lamb's quarters (*Chenopodium berlandieri*), which grows wild. It is also easy to grow, and seeds are widely available. It is sometimes sold at the farmer's market.

Queso Cotija

A semi-hard Mexican cheese originally from Michoacán. Can substitute ricotta salata or feta. We use cheese

in very small amounts. We prefer cheese made from pastured dairy animals. Cheese is never a critical component of our recipes and is used, instead, as a condiment. Vegans can get a creamy texture by using Cashew Crema (p. 183) or crumbles of vegan nut-based cheeses.

Queso Fresco

A soft young cheese. You can substitute paneer, farmer's cheese, or goat cheese.

Quinoa

Like amaranth, quinoa is commonly called a "grain" but is actually a highly nutritious seed. It was domesticated more than 4,000 years ago in the Andean region. Quinoa is related to *quelites*, as they are both in the *chenopodium* family. It sold in two forms: whole grain and flour.

Salt

According to the Mexica (Aztec) codices, eating food without chile was considered "fasting" and food without salt was considered "torture." Salt is an important flavor component in all cooking, not because it imparts a salty taste to food, but because it draws out the other flavors; a certain amount of salt (and each individual's taste for it is unique) is necessary to keep food from tasting bland. Develop your palate, taste your food, and adjust seasonings to achieve the desired effect. We recommend using unrefined sea salt instead of refined

iodized salt. We use salt mined from ancient sea beds in Utah. Before colonization, salt was highly valued and many native groups considered it sacred.

Shortening

In a few instances, our recipes call for small amounts of "non-hydrogenated" shortening. We believe the best choice is sustainably harvested, non-hydrogenated palm oil. For health reasons, we recommend avoiding all hydrogenated and partially hydrogenated oils and shortenings.

Tequesquite

Tequesquite is a natural alkaline mineral that has been used since pre-Conquest times as a leavening agent and flavoring for corn-based dishes such as tamales. It is mined from lakes in Central Mexico. It can be found at well-stocked Mexican markets and online (see Sources, p. 239).

Vanilla

Vanilla is derived from the seed pods of an orchid that originated in Mesoamerica and was cultivated by the Totonoc people of Papantla, Veracruz, thousands of years ago. Today, vanilla is most often used in extract form. Our recipes sometimes call for raw ground vanilla (ground seeds), which has a potent vanilla flavor without the alcohol used in extracts. It is expensive but keeps well, and a little goes a long way.

Verdolagas *(Portulaca oleracea)*

Commonly considered a weed, *verdolagas* grows in gardens and the cracks of sidewalks. Once you learn what it looks like, you'll see it everywhere. Known as purslane in English, it has become trendy; it's not unusual to see it served in salads and appetizers in high-end restaurants. Our ancestors usually ate it in stews or scrambled with eggs. Verdolagas are high in phytochemicals and omega-3 fatty acids. They help the body heal from wounds and injuries, and help the liver and kidneys heal from damage caused by medication and diabetes (respectively).

Xoconostle

This prickly pear cactus fruit *(Opuntia joconostle)* is sour, unlike other cactus fruits. The name literally means sour cactus: *xococ* ("something sour") and *nochtli* ("prickly pear"). Xoconostle are sold seasonally at well-stocked Mexican markets and are also available dried for purchase online (see Sources, p. 239).

Yerbaníz *(Tagetes lucida)*

In the pre-Conquest era, *yerbaníz* was used as medicine and as a flavoring for foods, including chocolate. Today, this plant has many names, including Mexican tarragon, Mexican Mint Marigold, grandmother plant, *pericón*, and others. It is easy to grow in warm-climate gardens. Dried leaves can be found in some well-stocked Mexican markets.

Tools

Molcajete/mortar and pestle

A *molcajete* is a mortar and pestle made of volcanic rock. *Molcajetes* have been used in the Americas for thousands of years. We love to use ours for grinding ingredients for salsa and for making guacamole. A mortar and pestle made of granite or other smooth stone is better for grinding spices. We use both.

Tortilla press

Used to press corn tortillas into even, flat discs. They are either made of wood, cast iron, or aluminum. You can find them online (see Sources p. 239) or in Mexican markets.

Airlock

Useful for fermentation of curtido, chile sauces, or brewing *tíbicos* (water kefir). Available and inexpensive at some stores with home-canning sections and widely available at stores specializing in home-brewing supplies. The most common is the S-shape, which has two small chambers that hold a small amount of water. An airlock releases air from the vessel without letting in additional air.

Citrus juicer

Called an *exprimidor* in Spanish, this hand tool is useful for juicing citrus, and it quickly produces more juice than squeezing the fruit by hand.

Slow cooker

This is an essential tool in our kitchen, because it allows us to cook foods (especially beans) over many hours when we're not available to watch the pot. Slow cookers (also known as crockpots) are available in a wide variety of brands, models, and prices. We prefer the kind that allows the crock to be removed from the heating element for cleaning. They can be purchased second-hand at a thrift store.

Cast iron griddle or *comal*

In pre-Conquest times, most food was cooked on a *comal*, a clay-fired griddle; now the term is also used for metal griddles. We find that cast iron produces a reliable, even heat. We use ours every day to make fresh tortillas, heat store-bought tortillas, make tlacoyos or sopes, toast dried chiles, and char fresh chiles, onions, and tomatoes.

Cooking Techniques...

These are tutorials for beginners. If you already have a tried-and-true method of cooking beans, roasting chiles, or making vegetable stocks, then by all means go ahead and do it your way. We don't claim to have the one "right way to do it," mainly because we don't really believe in one right way. This section is for people who don't already know how to do these things, or folks who don't like the results they're getting with the way they're already doing them.

COOKING BEANS

Food does not have to be fancy to be satisfying and tasty. Dried beans are inexpensive, tasty, and provide great fuel for your body. They're a core component of a decolonized diet for Mexican and Central American peoples. Coming home to the smell of a fresh pot of beans reminds us of visits to our grandmothers' homes. The simple act of cooking a pot of beans connects us to our ancestors, who for generations survived on a bean-rich diet. Once you start cooking your own beans, you'll find that they're more flavorful and economical than canned.

How to Cook Beans from Scratch

Begin by sorting the beans. Pour a handful onto a light-colored plate, and use your fingers to find anything that doesn't belong. Look for small pieces of debris

such as clumps of dirt or small pebbles and discard. Put the sorted beans in a pot or strainer, and go on to the next handful of beans. After all beans have been sorted, rinse them thoroughly in cool water. Dried beans are often quite dusty!

To Soak or Not to Soak:

People tend to have strong feelings about whether to soak beans before cooking. Some families have always soaked their beans and others never do. We soak our beans in water overnight because soaking can reduce cooking time by about 30 minutes and will reduce the amount of water needed by 1 cup (250 mL). Some people believe that soaking beans makes them easier to digest, while others argue that soaking beans diminishes their flavor. The recipes in this book do not include soaking time. If you decide to soak, you can use a little less liquid and cook for a little less time. To soak beans, put beans in a large pot. Add plenty of cool water (more than enough to cover) and let them sit 10–12 hours or overnight. Drain and use fresh water for cooking.

How to tell when beans are ready: Cooking times will vary depending on the beans used, so all times given in our recipes are ballpark figures. We have found that fresh beans cook more quickly than commodity beans that could be many years old. Organic and heirloom beans tend to be fresher than conventional beans, and those found at farmer's markets are much fresher than the ones from chain grocery stores.

In our opinion, it's very important that beans are not undercooked! They shouldn't be firm, and they shouldn't be al dente. Undercooked beans are more difficult to digest. The inside of the bean cooks quicker than the skin. We like our beans to have a soft and creamy texture, inside and out. We don't mind if a few of the beans begin to crack open, which is a sign that they're almost done.

Beans also vary in how much liquid (water or stock) they need to cook. We generally start with 6 cups (1 ½ L) to 1 lb (500 g) beans. Always keep a close eye on the beans as they cook and add more liquid as needed. Beans should float freely in the pot; without sufficient liquid, they'll cook unevenly. Even worse, they can burn.

When to add salt:

Salt is magic. It takes the beans from bland to "yum." Many cooks believe that adding salt to a pot of beans too early toughens the skins of the beans, while more recent research on this subject suggests that this is a myth. We usually add salt any time after the beans begin to "smell like beans." We use 2 tsp salt for every 1 lb (500 g) beans and then we taste and adjust.

Three Methods for Cooking Beans

We recommend three methods of cooking beans from scratch: 1) in a slow cooker; 2) in a pot on the stove; 3) in the oven. The bean recipes in this cookbook call for a slow cooker but can be easily adapted for any method. (Beans can also be cooked in a pressure cooker in about 30 minutes and with no advance preparation. We don't provide directions for this method because it is best used by cooks who are already familiar with pressure cookers.) Choose the method that works best for you.

1. Cooking Beans in a Slow Cooker

The slow cooker is a useful tool for those of us with busy schedules. A slow cooker allows us to come home after a long day at work to the smell of a delicious pot of fresh beans, which vastly decreases the urge to grab a quick dinner from a restaurant. If we are going to be gone all day, we always add more liquid to the pot than if we're going to be home to stir the beans and check the liquid level. Extra liquid can always be cooked off, drained off, or consumed.

Place rinsed and sorted beans, water or stock to cover, and any additional ingredients directly into the slow cooker (sometimes we'll sauté onions or garlic on the stove before adding them to the beans). Cook beans on high heat for anywhere from 4–6 hours or low heat

6–9 hours, or until the skins are soft and insides are creamy. Slow cookers vary greatly in their heat settings so you will need to experiment to find the right heat setting and amount of time necessary to cook a pot of beans in your own slow cooker. When we're in a hurry, we first boil the water in a teakettle before adding. We have friends who cook beans in a slow cooker overnight on low, and that works too.

Budget conscious tip:
Slow cookers can be found at thrift stores, garage sales, or swap meets. We have found that cheaper slow cookers work fine (and perhaps better than fancy ones!).

2. Cooking Beans on the Stove

Many of our friends will only cook their beans in a pot on the stove, because they believe this method produces the tastiest results. Place rinsed and sorted beans, along with water or stock and spices, in a large pot. One big advantage of this method is that you can quickly sauté the onions, garlic, and spices and then add beans and water to the same pot. Traditionally, clay pots were used to cook beans, but many cooks now use stainless steel or enameled cast-iron pots instead. Clay pots impart a subtle earthy flavor to the beans. (*Note:* If you use a clay pot for cooking, make sure it does not contain lead.)

In a large pot on high heat, bring beans to a soft boil, then reduce heat to medium-low. Beans should cook at a slow simmer. Continue to cook for 3–4 hours, or until beans begin to look soft. Check every so often and add water, if necessary, so they don't dry out or burn. When beans are soft, add salt and simmer on low heat for 20 minutes. Cooking beans on the stove produces the tastiest pot liquor. Some families serve bean pot liquor as a nutritional supplement to pregnant women, to elders, or to the ill—it's that good for you.

3. Cooking Beans in the Oven

This method is reliable, fast, and produces a very good tasting bean. Preheat oven to 350°F (168°C). In a 3 qt/L Dutch oven or other heavy cooking pot with tight-fitting lid on medium heat, sauté onions and garlic, if using. Add 1 lb (500 g) beans and water to cover by about 1 in (2.5 cm). Cover and bake for 90 minutes to 2 hours. Check the beans and add salt. If the beans are getting dry, add water as needed. Cook for 15 additional minutes or until the beans are soft and creamy. We find this is the fastest way to cook beans, aside from using a pressure cooker.

ROASTING GREEN CHILES

Roasted and peeled green chiles bring incredible flavor to any dish. While roasting chiles can be a chore, we have some tips to make it easier and more manageable.

Not all green chiles need to be roasted and peeled before eating or adding to recipes. In general, smaller chiles, like jalapeños and serranos, are eaten without peeling. The larger green varieties (Anaheim chiles, New Mexico green chiles, and poblano chiles) should always be roasted and peeled. In our recipes, they can be used interchangeably, although each will lend a slightly different flavor to your dish. The Anaheims have a bright clean taste with low heat. The flavor of New Mexico chiles is more robust and, while they vary in heat, even the mildest New Mexico chile is more flavorful than an Anaheim. Finally, poblanos have a deep, complex, and smoky flavor. The heat of all these chiles varies considerably depending on many factors, including where and under what conditions they were grown. For this reason, we recommend that you taste the chiles after roasting to determine how many to add to a dish. We have found that very fresh chiles—they are harvested at the very end of summer or early fall—are easiest to peel after roasting, so buy locally grown, in-season ones when you can.

There are three basic methods for roasting fresh chiles: broiled, stovetop, and grilled.

Broiled:

Rub chiles with a small amount of oil (coconut oil works great but use what you have). Spread them on a

baking sheet and place under a broiler. Watch carefully: when they start to turn black and blister, at about 5 minutes, turn them over using tongs. Continue to broil and turn until chiles are mostly blistered and blackened on all sides.

Stovetop:

Place chiles on a griddle on high heat. Once they start to char, turn them over. Continue to turn until they are mostly blackened and blistered on all sides. Some cooks use tongs to char the chiles directly over the flame of a gas stove. We find this works when you just need one chile, but is quite time-consuming when preparing many chiles at once.

Grilled:

We love to use our outdoor gas grill (a charcoal grill also works) to roast chiles. This method is quick and produces great results. Preheat grill on high. Rub chiles with oil and place them on the grill. Close the lid and roast for 5 minutes. Open lid and turn chiles over every 3–4 minutes until all sides are black and blistered.

After charring, place chiles in a bag or glass container with a tight lid to allow them to steam in their own heat for 30 minutes, which will help to release the outer skin. Working over a sink, carefully remove charred skin from the chile. Sometimes this is easy; other times, the skin is stubborn and you'll need to remove it in small pieces. After skin is removed, open chiles to remove seeds and, if desired, any large veins (the veins are often quite spicy). If you plan to use them for chiles rellenos, leave both ends intact. Using a sharp knife, carefully cut a slit lengthwise down one side.

Buying Roasted Chiles: A New Mexico Tradition

In New Mexico during chile season, roasted chiles are sold by the bushel in front of every grocery store. Families buy huge sacks and take them home, package them in freezer bags, and use the chiles throughout the year. Catriona's family has a long tradition of chile verde smuggling: After moving to California from New Mexico, they often made a pilgrimage to New Mexico during chile season, visiting the extended familia and always returning with a sack of fresh chiles that they concealed at the state border's agricultural checkpoint. Before freezing the chiles, they'd grill them on their backyard barbecue. Now we buy the green chiles already roasted and frozen and just bring them back in a cooler—no smuggling necessary.

ROASTING WINTER SQUASH

We love winter squash, including pumpkins. We grow them in the backyard and buy them at the farmer's

market. Although the fancy grocery stores sell them already cut up, it's a lot more expensive than buying the whole squash. Some of the large, hard-fleshed squashes can seem intimidating, and you might feel like you don't have a big enough knife to tackle the job. One solution we've found is to cook the squash before cutting and peeling: we bake it whole, seeds and all.

To roast a squash whole, remove middle or upper rack from the oven. Leave one rack near the bottom. Preheat oven to 375°F (190°C). Using a sharp knife, pierce the squash four or five times, just enough to let the steam escape. Place squash on a baking sheet, and bake for 60–90 minutes, until a knife can be easily inserted into the flesh. Allow squash to cool and cut in half. Remove the seeds. The skin should peel away easily from the flesh. If necessary, use a knife or peeler to help. Squash can be used right away or cubed and frozen for later use.

MAKING SOUP STOCKS

Using stock instead of water enhances the flavor of dishes. Our friends Margo and Hadas have taught us to store vegetable scraps in a container in the freezer until there are enough to make a batch of vegetable stock. The following scraps work great for stocks: carrots tops and peels, onion and garlic skins and scraps, leeks, celery, mushroom stems, corn cobs, stems from parsley and cilantro, potatoes, sweet potatoes, bell peppers, tomatoes, and squashes. Avoid cabbage, kale, and other brassicas as they can impart a bitter flavor.

To make stock, place 2 cups (500 mL) vegetable scraps in 6 cups (1 ½ L) water, along with a bay leaf and 6 peppercorns. Cook at a low simmer for at least 1 but preferably 3–6 hours. Cool and strain. Hadas's trick is to create a special stock for each recipe by featuring the flavors she wants to highlight, such as corn or garlic.

TOASTING & GRINDING SPICES

Spices add flavor, depth, and health benefits to a dish. To achieve maximum flavor, buy spices whole. Heat a small, dry frying pan on medium heat. Add spices; for example, cumin seeds, coriander seeds, or allspice. Shake the pan continuously for about 1 minute. You'll smell the fragrance release from the spices signaling you to remove them from heat and transfer to a mortar and pestle. Grind spices to a powder with the pestle. I find that adding just a little salt helps break down the spices with less effort. If a mortar and pestle is not available, use a spice or coffee grinder, taking care to clean it well before and after use. Another option is to put spices in a freezer bag and use a rolling pin to smash them into a powder. If pressed for time, use store-bought ground spices—just make sure they're fresh. In general, spices last about one year.

TAMALE DOUGH (MASA)

There are two ways to make masa (dough) for tamales. For Luz, the preferred method is to buy freshly made dough. Most areas with a significant Mexican immigrant population will have a *tortillería* (tortilla factory) or store that sells fresh masa. These businesses soak dried corn in slaked lime, also called cal, for 12 hours or longer; then they rinse and grind it. They do this every day and sell the freshly ground corn in various forms: "masa for tortillas" (a fine grind); "prepared masa for tamales" (a coarse grind with either lard or vegetable shortening and salt added); and "unprepared masa for tamales" with just the coarsely ground corn. We prefer to add our own shortening so that we can control the amount and quality. Fresh masa should be used right away, ideally the same day, but certainly within a few days.

The second method, which Catriona grew up with, is to make masa from the flour of nixtamalized corn, called masa harina. There are pros and cons for each method. Luz thinks fresh masa is less processed and produces superior results. However, fresh masa is most often made from conventionally grown corn; that made from organic and non-GM corn is only rarely available. Organic masa harina, on the other hand, is available in many locations and is widely available online. The more common brands of masa harina (those sold in Mexican markets) are not organic and are often made from genetically modified (GM) corn. Although corn grown in Mexico is not GM, thanks to the activism of peasant and indigenous groups, the mainstream brands, though Mexican, use US-grown corn.

Our recipes provide instructions for working with fresh masa. However, if fresh masa is not available or you want to use masa harina, follow these instructions.

TAMALES WITH MASA HARINA

1 cup (250 mL) non-hydrogenated shortening

1 tbsp sea salt

1 tbsp aluminum-free baking powder

4 ½ (1.1 L) cups masa harina

4 cups (1 L) warm water or stock (depending on recipe)

Using a hand or stand mixer, whip shortening for 5 minutes, or until double in size. Add salt and baking powder and whip into shortening. Add masa harina and water a little at a time, mixing after each addition until all ingredients have been incorporated. Put dough in a large bowl and hand knead. Masa will be sticky. As the dough is worked, the liquid will be absorbed and the masa will become less sticky.

IMPORTANT SHOPPING NOTE:

Make sure to buy masa harina or nixtamalized corn flour. Do not substitute regular corn meal or corn flour. Masa harina is sometimes labeled "instant corn masa."

MAKING NIXTAMAL

This last tutorial is not for beginners, but for those intrepid souls who, not satisfied with purchasing freshly ground masa or using masa harina, want to make their own from scratch so that they can choose the ingredients and see the process every step of the way. (See recipe on following page.) Even if you do this only once in your life, it's a great learning experience.

Nixtamal comes from the Nahuatl word *nixtamalli*, which means "unformed corn dough." Nixtamalization is the process of soaking dried corn in an alkaline solution, such as cal (calcium hydroxide) or wood ash. This soaking process makes the corn more digestible and the nutrients in the corn more accessible to the body. It also makes the corn easier to grind and to form into a dough (masa) for use in tortillas, tamales, pupusas, tlacoyos, and more. (To make pozole [hominy], you skip the grinding process and simply boil the nixtamal in water.) Nixtamal sustained our ancestors for thousands of years. No one knows for sure when they first discovered the process of nixtamalization—the earliest evidence was located in Guatemalan cooking equipment that is 3,500 years old! We think it quite powerful—at a spiritual and cultural level—to reclaim this practice.

NIXTAMAL

Allow 1 hour to prepare corn and 18–24 hours to soak.

6 cups (1 ½ L) water

2 tbsp cal (slaked lime)

2 cups (500 mL) dried field corn, any color, rinsed well

In a large non-reactive pot, whisk water with cal to create a slurry. Add corn. Cook on medium heat for 45 minutes, stirring occasionally and checking often. Ideally, water should just barely come to a slow boil at exactly 45 minutes. If it starts to look like it is about to boil before 45 minutes, reduce heat. If, at 30 minutes, it is not even close, increase heat. After 45 minutes, remove from heat and cover the pot. Allow corn to soak in pot overnight and preferably for about 24 hours.

Strain and rinse corn thoroughly under cool water. Put corn in a clean bowl and fill with clean, cool water. Working with a small amount at a time, rub corn vigorously between palms. The goal is to remove outer layer of skin (the hull), which should fall off pretty easily. Do not attempt to clean every single kernel, one at a time. It might seem like nothing is happening at first because the skin is pretty thin, but you should soon begin to see little bits of skin floating in the water. Pour off the top of the water along with the hulls that have been removed. Repeat this step about 10 times, until water poured off is almost completely clean. Rinse and strain the corn one last time. This nixtamal can now be used in pozole (p. 101), or you can grind it for use in tortillas, tamales, or tlacoyos. To grind nixtamal, use a *metate* or a manual-crank corn grinder. Some people have reported success using a food processor.

CHAPTER THREE

Antojitos: Appetizers & Snacks

CUCUMBER, JÍCAMA & MANGO STICKS

We think the Latina/o paradox is linked to the fact that Latin American immigrants eat so many fresh fruits and vegetables. In Latina/o neighborhoods, fruit vendor carts sell cups or baggies of fresh cut fruit with salt, lime, and chile. The sweet-sour-salty-hot flavors keep you wanting more.

....

Cut cucumbers, jícama, and mangos into strips about ¼ in (5 mm) wide and 4–5 in (10–12 cm) long. Squeeze juice of 1 lime on fruits and vegetables. Arrange in serving cups or margarita glasses. Sprinkle generously with Chile Lime Salt. Serve each with ¼ wedge of lime.

Chile Lime Salt

Preheat oven to 300°F (150°C).

Combine chiltepin chiles and zest in a mortar and use pestle to mash together until chiles are ground to a powder. Add salt, a bit at a time, and continue to mash to integrate the flavors. Add ground pasilla and mash to combine. Stir in lime juice. Place mixture in a small baking dish and bake for 12 minutes, stirring once, half-way through. Return mixture to mortar and mash one more time to break up clumps. Store any leftovers in an airtight container.

4 cucumbers, peeled and seeded

1 jícama, peeled

4 mangos, peeled

3 limes

Chile Lime Salt

8 dried chiltepin chiles (omit if you prefer a mild heat)

zest of 2 limes

2 tbsp sea salt

2 tbsp ground pasilla chile

1 tsp lime juice

makes 10–12 servings

AGUACHILE DE QUINOA

Aguachile is a traditional raw fish dish, popular in coastal regions. In this vegan version, we use quinoa instead of fish, but bathe it in the same spicy, bright, aromatic sauce. The spice of the chile is balanced with the tang of the lime juice, cooling cucumber, creamy avocado, and sweet mango. The combination is mouthwatering and addictive.

....

1 cup (250 mL) quinoa

½ tsp extra virgin coconut oil

½ tsp sea salt

½ cup (125 mL) fresh lime juice (about 5–6 juicy limes)

1 cucumber with peel, roughly chopped

1–3 jalapeños, stems and seeds removed

½ cup (125 mL) lightly packed cilantro

½ cup (125 mL) lightly packed parsley

¼ cup (60 mL) lightly packed fresh mint leaves

¼ cup (60 mL) lightly packed fresh lemon balm

½ tsp sea salt

⅛ tsp white pepper

1 cucumber, peeled and seeded

4 shallots, minced

2 avocados, peeled, seeded, and sliced

1 mango, peeled, seeded, and thinly sliced

⅓ cup (80 mL) cilantro leaves

kosher sea salt

10–12 corn tortillas to make Healthy Tostada Shells (p. 63), or store-bought shells

Rinse quinoa in a bowl of cold water and strain through a fine sieve. In a frying pan on medium heat, melt coconut oil. Add wet quinoa and toast until dry, about 3 minutes. Add 2 cups (500 mL) water and ½ tsp salt. Increase heat to high and bring mixture to a boil. Cover and reduce heat to low. Cook for 15 minutes, remove from heat, and allow mixture to rest for 5 minutes. Transfer to a large serving dish and fluff with a fork. Set aside until quinoa comes to room temperature.

In a blender or food processor, combine lime juice with chopped cucumber, 1 jalapeño, cilantro, parsley, mint, lemon balm, salt, and pepper, and purée until the consistency of juice. Add small amount of water if necessary to blend. Taste the liquid; it should be aggressively spicy. If necessary, add more jalapeños to bring up heat level. This recipe is best when the amount of chile provides the perfect balance between pain and pleasure. The bland quinoa will absorb heat, so liquid should start out very spicy.

Dice cucumber. Gently toss blended liquid with quinoa, cucumber, and shallots. Place a large mound of mixture on top of each tostada shell and garnish with a few slices each of avocado and mango, cilantro leaves, and a sprinkle of salt.

Healthy Tostada Shells:

10–12 tortillas

Preheat oven to 400°F (200°C). Put tortillas on 2–3 cookie sheets, without overlapping. If necessary, work in batches. Bake tortillas for 17 minutes or until crispy, turning over at the halfway point.

SUBSTITUTIONS:

Although this version uses mint and lemon balm, experiment using other combinations of fresh herbs: basil or Mexican herbs, such as pápalo *or* pipicha, *all work well. If only cilantro and parsley are available, increase proportions slightly.*

makes 12 servings

1 large head cauliflower

1 bunch cilantro

1 small white onion, coarsely chopped

1–3 fresh jalapeño chiles, to taste

2 garlic cloves, peeled

3 tomatoes, diced

⅓ cup (80 mL) lime juice

¾ tsp sea salt

⅛ tsp white pepper

12–14 Healthy Tostada Shells (p. 63), a large bag of tortilla chips, or 12–14 butter lettuce leaves

2 avocados, peeled, seeded, and cubed

CEVICHE DE COLIFLOR (CAULIFLOWER CEVICHE)

Inspired by the fresh taste of traditional ceviche made with raw fish, this vegan version serves the same bold flavors—lime juice and chile—and is perfect to take to a potluck or serve as an appetizer or snack. Even folks who don't eat cauliflower will rave! Luz's student Alberto taught us that using a food processor with this recipe produces a perfect mince, but if you don't have one, a sharp knife will work just as well.

....

Working in batches, use a food processor to mince cauliflower, cilantro, onion, chiles, and garlic. Don't try to process too much in one batch. Process until vegetables are pea-sized, or use a sharp knife to mince. Transfer to a salad bowl and toss with tomatoes, lime juice, salt, and pepper. Cover and refrigerate for 1 hour before serving.

Serve on tostada shells, with tortilla chips, or in lettuce cups. Top with cubes of avocado.

makes 12 sopes

2 tbsp extra virgin coconut oil

1 tsp achiote seeds

2 lb (900g) fresh masa for tortillas or 2 cups (500 mL) masa harina mixed with 1 ½ cups (375 mL) hot water

1 onion, diced

½ tsp dried thyme

8 oz (230 g) maitake mushrooms, chopped

1 cup (250 mL) organic corn kernels, fresh if in season, otherwise frozen

½ tsp sea salt

⅛ tsp pepper

¼ cup (60 mL) cilantro leaves

Chiltepinera Hot Sauce (p. 173) or store-bought hot sauce

SOPES WITH MAITAKE MUSHROOMS & CORN

Sopes are round corn masa cakes with a pinched rim to hold a filling. Our filling combines delicious and medicinal maitake mushrooms with fresh sweet corn and thyme.

....

Preheat oven to 350°F (180°C).

In a small frying pan on medium heat, melt coconut oil and add achiote seeds. Cook for 5 minutes, stirring often. Do not let seeds burn. Transfer oil and seeds to a small heatproof cup and set aside.

Divide masa into 12 balls, each about the size of a golf ball. Using hands, form ball into flat disc about 3 ½ in (9 cm) in diameter. Gently pinch edges up to form a lip about ⅓ in (just under 1 cm) high.

Preheat a cast-iron griddle on high. Reduce heat to medium and place flat side of sope on griddle. Cook until it turns a toasty color, about 3–5 minutes. Turn over and cook for about 1 minute, taking care not to burn edges. Continue to cook sopes.

Brush sopes on all sides with a small amount of coconut oil and place on a cookie sheet, flat side down. Bake for 25 minutes.

Strain achiote oil and discard seeds. In a frying pan on medium, heat achiote oil and sauté onions until almost caramelized. Add thyme and mushrooms and sauté for 10 minutes. Add corn and sauté for 3 minutes. Season with salt and pepper. To serve, fill sopes with mushroom mixture and top with a few cilantro leaves and hot sauce.

Left to right: Sopes with Maitake Mushrooms & Corn, Ancho Chiles Stuffed with Guacamole (p. 70)

makes 2 cups (500 mL)

CLASSIC GUACAMOLE

1 fresh serrano chile, stems and seeds removed and minced

¼ white onion, minced

4 ripe avocados, peeled, seeded, and cubed

¼ cup (60 mL) chopped cilantro

1 tsp lime juice

½ tsp sea salt

⅛ tsp white pepper

The name comes from the Nahuatl words aguacatl (avocado) and molli (paste). Guacamole brings together avocado's rich creaminess with the zest of lime juice and the slight kick of chile. Serve it as an appetizer or snack, add to dishes as a condiment, or smear on a tortilla for a quick, light meal.

....

Using a *molcajete* or a small salad bowl and fork, mash chile and onion to break down slightly. Add cubes of avocado and smash, leaving some chunks. Gently stir in remainder of ingredients. Taste and adjust seasonings, if necessary.

SUPER-CHARGED GUACAMOLE

Spirulina and chia seeds were important foods for the Mexica (Aztec) people, providing complete protein and sustained energy. We've developed this recipe to incorporate these foods into our own diet, as they contain many life-giving properties. Guacamole is the ideal vehicle to provide healthy vegetable fats and is a hearty and delicious snack.

....

Using a *molcajete* or a small salad bowl and fork, mash chile and onions to break down slightly. Add avocado cubes and spirulina. Mash vigorously to distribute spirulina evenly throughout. Gently stir in remainder of ingredients. Taste and adjust seasonings.

1 fresh serrano chile, stems and seeds removed and minced

¼ white onion, minced

4 ripe avocados, peeled, seeded, and cubed

½ tsp raw spirulina powder

¼ cup (60 mL) chopped cilantro

1 tsp lime juice

1 tsp chia seeds

½ tsp sea salt

⅛ tsp white pepper

makes 6 servings

4 garlic cloves, peeled and
smashed

5 allspice berries

½ tsp sea salt

1 cup (250 mL) Pineapple
Vinegar (p. 177) or apple
cider vinegar

1 small cone piloncillo (about
1 oz [30 gr])

6 dried ancho chiles

Classic Guacamole (p. 68)

4 oz (115 grams) queso fresco
or ½ cup Cashew Crema
(p. 183)

ANCHO CHILES STUFFED WITH GUACAMOLE

This dish looks complicated, but the technique of rehydrating dried red chiles in a bath of vinegar, honey, and spices is actually quite simple. We serve them at room temperature when stuffed with guacamole, but we also enjoy hot fillings, such as refried beans, mashed sweet potatoes with garlic, or a mixture of quinoa and vegetables.

....

In a saucepan on high heat, cook garlic, allspice, salt, vinegar, 1 ½ cups (625 mL) water, and *piloncillo* for about 5 minutes, or until mixture comes to a slow boil. Stir to melt *piloncillo*.

On a griddle on medium heat, toast chiles for about 1 minute per side.

Remove liquid from heat and add chiles, using a small plate to keep submerged. Allow chiles to soak in liquid for 20 minutes, turning over and rearranging every 5 minutes so that they soak evenly on all sides.

Carefully remove chiles from liquid and use a sharp knife to make a single slit in each chile from stem to point. Carefully remove seeds and veins, leaving stem intact if possible. Place chiles on a large serving dish and fill with guacamole. Serve garnished with crumbled *queso fresco*.

MAMA CHITLE'S HEALTHY POPCORN SNACK

Popcorn is a quick and delicious whole grain snack, full of antioxidants. It originated in Peru about 6,700 years ago and was known in the Mexica (Aztec) empire as momochitl. Enjoy this nutty fruity snack mix, but be warned: you and your guests will devour it by the handful! (Adapted from E. Barrie Kavasch, Enduring Harvests: Native American Foods and Festivals for Every Season.*)*

....

Preheat oven to 325°F (160°C).

In a large pot with a tight-fitting lid on medium-high, heat oil. Place 3 popcorn kernels in pot, and when 1 has popped, remove them and pour in rest of popcorn and cover. Once you hear popping, shake pan often. After 1 minute, gently open lid slightly to allow a bit of steam to escape. When popping slows, remove pan from heat. When popping stops, carefully remove lid and immediately transfer popcorn into a large salad bowl. Remove any un-popped kernels. Season with salt and pepper.

Spread nuts and seeds on a rimmed cookie sheet or shallow pan. Bake for 14 minutes. In a small saucepan on medium, heat maple syrup and cinnamon for 5 minutes, stirring constantly with a wooden spoon. Remove mixture from heat and gently stir in nuts, seeds, and raisins, stirring until lightly coated in warm maple syrup. Pour mixture over popcorn. Use salad tongs to combine. Taste and season with salt and pepper, if desired.

¼ cup (60 mL) extra virgin coconut oil

⅔ cup (160 mL) organic popcorn

½ tsp sea salt

¼ tsp pepper

1 cup (250 mL) shelled peanuts

½ cup (125 mL) shelled pecans, chopped

½ cup (125 mL) raw, hulled sunflower seeds

½ cup (125 mL) raw, hulled pumpkin seeds

⅓ cup (80 mL) pure maple syrup

½ tsp ground cinnamon, preferably Ceylon or *canela Mexicana*

½ cup (125 mL) raisins

makes 4 servings

SPICY SALTY PEANUTS

1 tsp extra virgin coconut oil

8 dried chiles de árbol

1 cup (250 mL) raw unsalted, shelled peanuts

8 garlic cloves, peeled (if large, halved lengthwise)

½ tsp sea salt

3 dried chiltepin chiles, ground into a fine powder

High in protein, peanuts are a healthy snack. Thought to have originated in Peru or Brazil, peanuts were present in Mexico at the time of the Conquest, evidence of pre-colonial trading. This traditional snack has that perfect balance of salt and chile. You can adjust the heat to your liking by adding more or fewer chiltepin chiles.

....

In a frying pan on medium-low, heat oil. Add chiles de árbol and, using a wooden spoon, stir until coated in oil. Add peanuts and garlic, continuing to stir to prevent burning. Reduce heat when peanuts begin to brown. Cook for 5–6 minutes, or until garlic is cooked through. Remove from heat and add salt and ground chiltepin. Stir to combine and place in a serving bowl. At this point, having imparted their flavor, chiles de árbol serve only as a garnish and should not be eaten.

CHAPTER FOUR

Ensaladas: Salads

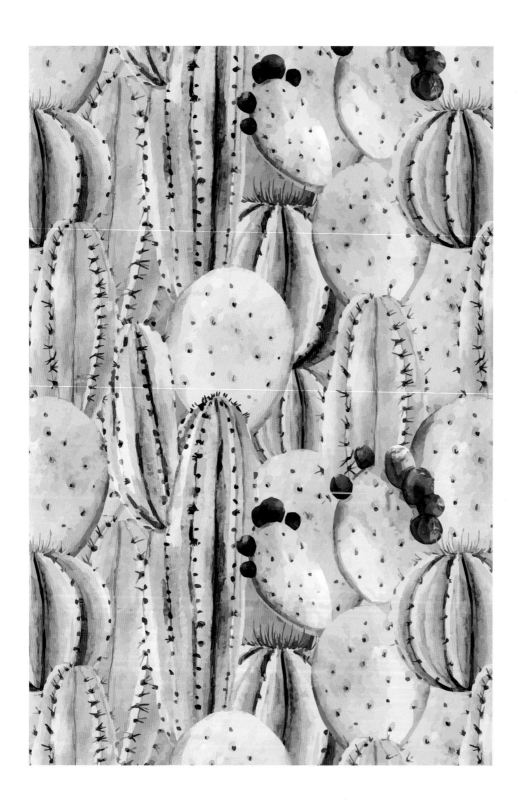

CLASSIC NOPALITO SALAD

This recipe is a good place to start for those new to nopales (cactus paddles). The cooking method removes much of the gel, yielding a salad that's fresh, clean, and a bit spicy. We're big believers in the multiple health benefits of nopales, a staple of the Mexican countryside. This recipe has a Sonoran twist, using chiltepin chiles to give quick, clean heat. (Inspired by "Sonora Desert Nopales Salad" in Marilyn Tausends's Cocina De La Familia.*)*

....

In a large pot on high, cover diced nopales with cold water and bring to a boil for 5 minutes. Drain, rinse well, and repeat with fresh water, onions, and sprigs of cilantro. Simmer for 10–15 minutes or until tender. Strain and rinse well in cold water. This process will remove most of the slippery texture sometimes associated with nopales. Remove onions and cilantro pieces and compost them.

In a salad bowl, toss nopales, oil, garlic, onion rings, tomatoes, chopped cilantro, and oregano. Sprinkle with lime juice, chiltepin chiles, and just enough olive oil to coat. Season with salt and pepper to taste. Let stand at room temperature for 20 minutes to allow flavors to meld.

SUBSTITUTION:

If chiltepin chiles are not available, use 1 fresh serrano or jalapeño, minced. If fresh nopales are not available, use 1 28-oz (796-mL) jar canned nopales.

- 6 nopal paddles, cleaned, spines removed, and diced
- 1 tbsp extra virgin olive oil
- ½ white onion
- 5 cilantro sprigs
- 1 garlic clove, peeled and finely minced
- ½ white onion, cut into very thin rings
- 1 pint (500 mL) cherry tomatoes, halved
- ¼ cup (60 mL) chopped cilantro leaves
- 1 tsp dried oregano, preferably Mexican
- 1 tbsp fresh lime juice
- 2 dried chiltepin chiles, ground
- 3 tbsp extra virgin olive oil
- ¼ tsp or more sea salt
- freshly ground black pepper
- ¼ lb (125 g) crumbled queso fresco (optional)

Aug 18, 17: too many onions

NOPALES "DE COLORES" SALAD

6 nopal paddles, cleaned,
  spines removed

2 fresh poblano chiles

about 1 tbsp extra virgin
  coconut oil

2–3 ears of corn, to make 2 cups
  (500 mL) kernels

1 orange bell pepper

½ red onion, finely diced

seeds of 1 pomegranate
  (optional, if in season)

4 oz (115 g) crumbled *queso
  cotija* (optional)

Vinaigrette

1 garlic clove

¼ tsp sea salt

2 tbsp red wine vinegar

⅛ tsp white pepper

4 tbsp extra virgin olive oil

In the United Farm Workers' movement, the folk song "De Colores" uses the image of multiple colors to signal appreciation for biodiversity in the fields, in the people, and in the beauty of creation. We use this principle in creating this dish because we strive to eat fruits and vegetables of every color each day. Get your "five a day" in this zesty grilled salad, while at the same time benefitting from the blood sugar-stabilizing properties of the cactus. This is best prepared in the fall, when the vegetables are freshly harvested.

....

Heat a grill (or grill pan) to medium-high heat. Lightly coat nopal paddles and poblano chiles in coconut oil. Shuck and clean corn. Place nopales, poblanos, whole bell pepper, and corn on grill. Cook for about 5 minutes and then turn. Continue to cook until each vegetable is cooked through, about 15–20 minutes. Remove corn when just slightly charred on all sides. Poblanos and bell pepper need to be thoroughly charred. When vegetables are sufficiently cooked or charred, remove from grill and set aside.

Place poblano and bell pepper in a covered bowl and allow to steam for 20 minutes. When cool, slip them out of their skins and remove seeds and stems. Cut into ¼-in (6-mm) wide strips and then cut strips about 2–3 in (5–8 cm) long. Cut nopales to same measurement. Using a sharp knife, cut corn kernels from cob.

To make vinaigrette, place garlic and salt in a mortar and use pestle to grind to a smooth paste. Add vinegar and pepper and let rest for about 10 minutes, while preparing salad. To finish vinaigrette, whisk in olive oil.

In a salad bowl, gently combine nopales, bell peppers, poblanos, corn kernels, and onions with pomegranate seeds. Pour vinaigrette over salad and toss to combine. Taste and adjust seasonings. Serve salad at room temperature, garnished, if desired, with crumbled *queso cotija*.

PACHAMAMA GREEN SALAD

1 small garlic clove, peeled

⅛ tsp sea salt

freshly ground black pepper

1 tbsp red wine vinegar

3–4 tbsp avocado oil

2 small heads butter lettuce, washed in cold water

¼ small jícama, peeled and cut in matchsticks

1 avocado, peeled, seeded, and cubed

2 tbsp roasted and salted sunflower seeds

¼ cup (60 mL) edible flowers (see note below)

In 2010, Bolivia passed a Law of the Rights of Mother Earth that reflects the indigenous Andean concept of Pachamama as a living being. The law states: "She [Pachamama] is in permanent balance, harmony and communication with the cosmos." This salad celebrates the bounty and the beauty of Pachamama, reminding us to respect and honor her. Edible flowers, tender greens, crunchy jícama, and creamy avocado bring together beauty, flavor, and health in each bite.

....

In a mortar and pestle, mash together garlic, salt, and pepper. Add vinegar and use pestle to create a thin paste, breaking down garlic as much as possible. Using a fork or small whisk, slowly whisk in oil. Set vinaigrette aside to rest for 5 minutes. Tear lettuce into bite-sized pieces, removing crunchy parts of stems, as desired. Thoroughly toss lettuce greens and jícama with vinaigrette. Add avocado and gently toss. Sprinkle with sunflower seeds and edible flowers.

Our favorite edible flowers are nasturtiums, borage, violas, johnny-jump-ups, calendula, arugula, and chives. Smaller flowers can be kept whole, but for larger flowers, use just petals.

VAMPIRO BEET & CARROT SALAD

The vampiro (vampire) is a refreshing, bright red, fresh juice made from carrots, beets, and oranges. It's credited with curing all kinds of ills, from anemia to hangovers. Our vampiro salad is inspired by the potency of this curative juice. It's a vivid show-stopper, and you won't believe how sweet it is!

....

In a small jar with a tight-fitting lid, combine orange and lime juice, vinegar, salt, pepper, maple syrup, and jalapeño. Shake to combine. Add olive oil and shake well. Toss carrots with half of dressing. Toss beets with remainder of dressing. To plate each serving, place a scoop of beets next to carrots for a beautiful contrast of pink and orange. Garnish with mint and serve with lime wedge.

4 tbsp freshly squeezed orange juice

2 tbsp freshly squeezed lime juice

1 tsp red wine vinegar

1 tsp sea salt

¼ tsp white pepper

1 tsp pure maple syrup

1 tbsp fresh jalapeño, minced

2 tbsp extra virgin olive oil

2 cups (500 mL) grated carrots (about 4 large carrots)

2 cups (500 mL) grated beets (about 3 beets)

20 mint leaves, sliced into thin ribbons

1 lime, quartered

KICK-ASS CHAYOTE SALAD WITH PICKLED RED ONIONS

This simple, colorful salad is a nutritional powerhouse. The crunchy chayote is high in antioxidant phytochemicals that may help undo some of the damage caused by the Standard American Diet. This salad has benefits for all ages: the folate in the chayote is especially good for pregnant moms and for the brain health of our elders. Mint is an especially potent inhibitor of cancer cells.

....

Using a potato peeler, remove green skin from chayotes. (If chayotes irritate your skin, wear rubber gloves.) Slice chayotes lengthwise, remove seed, and dice. Place diced chayotes, corn kernels, tomatoes, and cilantro in a bowl and gently toss. To prepare dressing, whisk together lime juice, mustard, honey, salt, and pepper. Slowly drizzle in olive oil while continuing to whisk. Stir in mint and jalapeño. Lightly dress salad and garnish with pickled red onions.

3 chayotes

2–3 ears of corn, to make 2 cups (500 mL) kernels (fresh if in season, otherwise frozen and parboiled)

1 pint (500 mL) cherry tomatoes, halved

1 bunch cilantro, stems removed and chopped

¼ cup (60 mL) lime juice

1 tsp organic stoneground mustard

½ tsp raw local honey

⅛ tsp sea salt

freshly ground pepper, to taste

¼ cup (60 mL) extra virgin olive oil

¼ cup (60 mL) chopped fresh mint

1 fresh jalapeño, finely minced

1 Pickled Red Onion (p. 180)

makes 4–6 servings

2 heads butter lettuce, washed
  and dried

zest of 1 lime

1 tbsp lime juice

5 tbsp avocado oil

⅛ tsp sea salt

2 crisp nectarines cut in thin
  wedges

¼ red onion, very thinly sliced
  and separated

2 red radishes, very thinly sliced

salt, to taste

¼ cup (60 mL) fresh purslane
  leaves

freshly ground pepper, to taste

2 oz (60 g) crumbled fresh goat
  cheese (optional)

4–6 nasturtium flowers
  (optional)

VERDOLAGAS & NECTARINE SUMMER SALAD

Humble purslane, a weed that grows in the cracks of urban sidewalks, is now featured on the menus of the fanciest restaurants. Our abuelitas (grandmothers) knew this plant as verdolagas in Spanish, harvesting it for use in stews. Lemony and slightly succulent, purslane is a powerful medicine, especially for diabetics whose organs may be severely stressed.

....

Gently tear lettuce into bite-sized pieces. In a jar with a tight-fitting lid, shake to combine lime zest, lime juice, oil, and salt. Toss lettuce, nectarine, onions, radishes, and a few pinches of salt. Dress salad with just enough dressing to lightly coat. Divide salad onto serving plates. Scatter purslane leaves on top of each salad. Season with freshly ground pepper. If desired, garnish each salad with a bit of goat cheese and/or a nasturtium flower.

WATERCRESS & STRAWBERRY SALAD WITH SERRANO VINAIGRETTE

makes 4 servings

2 tbsp homemade fruit or red wine vinegar

1 shallot, minced

¼ fresh serrano chile, minced

1 tbsp Dijon mustard

¼ tsp sea salt

1 tsp pure maple syrup

¼ cup avocado oil

¼ cup (60 mL) pine nuts

1 bunch watercress, stems removed

2 cups (500 mL) baby arugula

2 cups (500 mL) sliced strawberries

Watercress is known as berro in Mexico, and frequently used in fresh salads. It's is a cruciferous vegetable, especially good for fighting and preventing breast cancer. This is a bright, piquant salad with a bold vinaigrette complementing sweet strawberries and earthy pine nuts.

....

Put vinegar, shallots, and serrano in a small jar with a tight-fitting lid. Shake and allow to rest for 5 minutes to mellow out the shallots and allow chile to infuse dressing. Add mustard and salt and shake well to emulsify. Add maple syrup and oil and shake to combine.

In a dry frying pan on medium heat, toast pine nuts for three minutes, or until they just begin to brown. Remove immediately from pan and set aside.

Combine watercress, arugula, and strawberries in a salad bowl and gently toss with vinaigrette. Sprinkle pine nuts over salad.

TEPARY BEAN SALAD

We really like bean salads in the summer, especially at the end of hot summer days, when you can't face a hot and heavy entrée. Tepary beans are slightly sweet and nutty, and have a lower glycemic index than most other beans. This salad is satisfying, sustaining, and—with the jalapeño—a little bit sassy. Leftovers are great for lunch the next day.

....

2 cups (500 mL) white or brown tepary beans

1 heaping tsp dried oregano, preferably Mexican

1 heaping tsp epazote

3 garlic cloves, chopped

2 tsp sea salt

¼ cup extra virgin olive oil

1 tsp ground cumin

2 garlic cloves, finely chopped

2 celery stalks, finely diced

1 bunch green onions, including greens, diced

1 red bell pepper, finely diced

1 carrot, scrubbed and finely diced

1–2 fresh jalapeños, minced, to taste

2 tbsp fresh lime juice

½ cup (125 mL) chopped fresh cilantro

¼ tsp black pepper

1 tsp–1 tbsp red wine vinegar, to taste

½ tsp sea salt, to taste

Rinse and sort beans. In a slow cooker, combine 6 cups (1 ½ mL) water, beans, oregano, epazote, garlic, and salt. Cook beans on high heat for 4–6 hours or low heat 6–9 hours. (Tepary beans may take longer to cook than other beans.) For this salad, beans should be soft but not broken. Strain and gently rinse beans in cool water and place them in a large salad bowl.

In a small heavy frying pan on medium-low, heat oil. Add cumin and garlic. Remove from heat and tilt pan, stirring, until fragrance is released and garlic is cooked but not burnt, 30–60 seconds. Quickly pour over tepary beans and toss to combine. Add in remainder of ingredients and toss again. Add red wine vinegar and salt last, tasting as you go. Vinegar should bring a pleasant acidity to the dish, making the flavors pop.

SUBSTITUTIONS:

If tepary beans are not available, use white or navy beans.
In a rush? You can use canned beans.

COLORFUL FRUIT SALAD

makes 6 servings

This bright salad is a bowl full of sunshine and color. It's a quick and easy snack, dessert, or potluck contribution that will make everyone smile. We always make extra, because it seems to inspire a lot of nibbling in the kitchen.

....

In a small saucepan on medium heat, combine lime juice, water, honey, basil leaves with stems, and salt. Bring to a simmer and cook for 5 minutes, allowing mixture to reduce. Remove from heat and cool to room temperature. Remove basil leaves. Arrange fruit on a serving platter. Drizzle with honey-lime syrup and sprinkle with chia seeds. Garnish with basil leaves.

SUBSTITUTION:

If prickly pear fruits are not available, use 1 pint (500 mL) fresh strawberries, hulled and sliced.

¼ cup (60 mL) lime juice

¼ cup (60 mL) water

2 tbsp raw local honey

3 basil leaves, including thick stems

⅛ tsp sea salt

6 red prickly pear fruits (tunas), peeled and cut into rounds

½ Mexican papaya, peeled, seeded, and cut into bite-sized wedges

½ pineapple, peeled, cored, and cut into bite-sized wedges

1 tsp chia seeds (optional)

6 basil leaves, sliced into thin ribbons

CHAPTER FIVE

Sopas y Guisados: Soups & Stews

CHICOMECOATL CORN SOUP

Eating this elegant soup is like getting a warm embrace from Chicomecoatl, the goddess of ripe corn. We love the way sweet corn and roasted chiles taste together. This soup is best in mid-summer when fresh, organic corn is plentiful at farmer's markets and roadside stands. (Adapted from Martin Jacobs and Beverly Cox, Spirit of the Earth: Native Cooking from Latin America.*)*

....

Preheat oven to 375°F (190°C).

Spread corn kernels in a single layer on 2 baking sheets. Roast until edges begin to turn golden brown, 10–15 minutes. If using frozen corn, it probably won't brown on edges, so just roast for 15 minutes to concentrate flavors.

In a large pot on medium heat, melt butter. Add onions and sauté until translucent, about 10 minutes. Add ½ chile, garlic, and 1 cup (250 mL) corn kernels. Cook, stirring often, for 3–4 minutes.

In a blender, purée remainder of 3 cups (750 mL) corn along with tomato and 2 cups (500 mL) corn stock. Add purée, remainder of stock, 1 tbsp chopped cilantro, salt, and pepper. Taste and add more chiles if desired. Poblanos are usually quite mild, but every now and then you might find a hot batch. This soup is meant to have a mild heat to balance the sweetness of the corn. Bring soup to a slow boil, reduce heat to medium, and simmer for 20 minutes, stirring occasionally. Taste and adjust seasonings. Garnish each bowl with a sprig of cilantro.

6–7 ears of corn, to make 6 cups (1 ½ L) kernels (fresh if in season, otherwise frozen)

4 tbsp butter, preferably pastured

1 white onion, diced

½–3 fresh poblano chiles, roasted, peeled, seeded, and diced

3 garlic cloves, peeled and minced

1 large heirloom tomato, preferably orange or yellow, cored

6 cups (1 ½ L) corn stock (see p. 90)

1 tbsp chopped cilantro

1 tsp sea salt

¼ tsp white pepper

6 cilantro sprigs

CORN STOCK

I. USING CORN COBS:

This method uses corn cobs from which the kernels have been removed to create a stock with the flavor and aroma of fresh corn.

....

6 corn cobs, halved

1 onion, quartered (optional)

4 peppercorns (optional)

1 bay leaf (optional)

fresh herb sprigs (thyme, parley, Mexican mint marigold, epazote, or cilantro) (optional)

In a large pot on high heat, add corn cobs to 8 cups (2 L) water. Add remainder of ingredients if desired and bring to a boil. Reduce heat to low and simmer for 1–2 hours. Strain and compost solids. Refrigerate or freeze stock if not using right away.

2. USING CORN SILK:

Corn silk is good for urinary health, blood pressure, and inflammation. People with diabetes, low potassium levels, or pregnant moms should check with their health care provider or herbalist before using corn silk tea.

....

1 oz (30 g) corn silk (or silk from 2–3 ears of corn)

In a large pot on high heat, boil corn silk in 4 cups (1 L) water for 5 minutes. Remove from heat and steep for 20 minutes.

CHIPOTLE PUMPKIN SOUP ALCHEMY

We call this soup "alchemy" because the ingredients make magic together. Rich and creamy, it is a perfect soup for winter months. Chipotle adds a smoky note, but use only a little (even if you think you're tough!). Cinnamon adds flavor complexity and helps regulate blood glucose levels.

....

If using fresh pumpkin, prepare according to cooking techniques, pp. 54–55. If using squash, roughly chop after it has been roasted, peeled, and seeded.

In a large pot on medium-high heat, sauté onions in oil for 5–6 minutes, stirring often. Add garlic, cumin, coriander, and 1 tbsp chipotle. Stir to combine and cook for 1 minute. Add pumpkin, cinnamon stick, vegetable stock, oregano, and salt. Bring to a simmer, then reduce heat to medium-low, and cook for 30 minutes.

In a dry, hot frying pan on high heat, toast pumpkin seeds until they start to puff up or turn brown, about 3 minutes. Remove pumpkin seeds from pan and set aside.

Remove cinnamon stick from soup. With an immersion blender, purée soup until creamy or, working in batches, use a blender. (Be careful when blending hot liquids!) Cover blender lid with a folded dishtowel and hold in place. Pulse once and open blender to allow steam to escape. Repeat this process twice and then begin to blend starting on low and building up to high speed. If soup is too thick, add water, a little at a time. Return soup to pot, and add lime juice and maple syrup. Taste and adjust seasonings. For a spicier soup, add more chipotle en adobo. Adjust levels of spice, salt, acid, and sweet until soup has the perfect balance between these elements. (Cooking is magic and alchemy.) Serve in bowls, each garnished with toasted pumpkin seeds, a cilantro leaf, and Cashew Crema (p. 183).

7 lb (3.15 kg) cooking pumpkin, winter squash, or 3 15-oz (425-g) cans pumpkin purée

1 white onion, chopped

2 tbsp extra virgin coconut oil

4 garlic cloves, chopped

1 tsp cumin seeds, toasted and ground in mortar and pestle

1 tsp coriander seeds, toasted and ground in mortar and pestle

1–2 tbsp Chipotles en Adobo (p. 167) or canned, minced

1 cinnamon stick, preferably Ceylon or canela Mexicana

4–6 cups (1 L–1 ½ L) vegetable stock

1 tsp dried oregano, preferably Mexican

1 tsp sea salt, more to taste

¼ cup (60 mL) raw, hulled pumpkin seeds (pepitas)

1 tbsp lime juice

½ tsp pure maple syrup

6 leaves cilantro

½ cup Cashew Crema (p. 183) (optional)

PURÉPECHA BEAN SOUP

makes 8–10 servings

The ancient Purépecha people were excellent strategists and fierce warriors: they dealt one of the few major defeats to the powerful Mexica (Aztec) armies. Today, the Purépecha, located in the Mexican state of Michoacán, continue their tradition of struggle and are active in resisting illegal logging and clear-cutting of their forests. This recipe honors their resilience: a velvety soup garnished with crispy corn tortillas and chewy, bittersweet strips of ancho chiles.

....

2 cups (500 mL) dried beans
  (bayo, Flor de Mayo,
  Mayocoba, or pinto)

2 tsp sea salt

2 dried pasilla chiles

4 tomatoes

4 garlic cloves

1 onion, peeled and quartered

5 corn tortillas

1 tbsp olive oil

¼ tsp salt

3 dried ancho chiles

about ¼ cup (60 mL) extra
  virgin coconut oil

2 ripe avocados, peeled,
  seeded, sliced

1 cup (250 mL) crumbled queso
  fresco

CONTINUED ▶

In a slow cooker, add 6 cups (1 ½ L) water to rinsed and sorted beans and cook until tender on high heat for 4–6 hours, or low heat for 6–9 hours. When beans are almost cooked, add salt. When beans are soft, use an immersion blender to blend into a purée (or, working in batches, purée in a food processor or blender).

Rinse pasilla chiles in cold water and pat dry with a clean towel. On a medium-hot griddle, cook chiles for about 1 minute on each side, taking care not to burn. Put chiles in a bowl, cover with boiling water, and let soak for 30 minutes. Remove stems and seeds and put chiles in blender.

On a very hot dry griddle, cook tomatoes, garlic, and onions until they just begin to blacken on all sides. Remove peels from garlic. Core tomato. Add tomatoes, onions, and garlic to blender (along with chiles) and blend for about 1 minute. If necessary to aid blending, add a bit of water.

In a large pot on medium heat, add chile purée and cook for 10 minutes. Stir in bean purée and bring mixture to a slow boil. Reduce heat to low and simmer for 30 minutes, stirring occasionally, to allow flavors to meld.

▶▶ To make tortilla strips: Preheat oven to 400°F (200°C). Cut tortillas in half, then crosswise into 1/4-in (6-mm) strips. Put tortillas in a mixing bowl. Slowly drizzle in olive oil while tossing. Sprinkle salt on tortillas and toss to combine. Spread strips over a cookie sheet and bake for 15 minutes, turning after 8 minutes. Set aside.

To make chile strips: Cut off top stems and slice open ancho chiles. Wash chiles well to remove seeds and dust, then thoroughly pat dry. (*Chiles should be completely dry.*) Using kitchen shears or a sharp knife, cut chiles lengthwise into thin strips, at most 1/8-in (3-mm) thick. Cut long strips in half. In a small frying pan on medium heat, melt coconut oil so that it is about 1/4-in (6-mm) deep. Be ready with tongs and a paper towel spread out near stove. When oil is hot (almost shimmering), quickly add chile strips and use tongs to coat in oil. After 10–15 seconds, remove from heat and as quickly as possible remove strips from oil and set to drain on paper towel. *Note: chile strips will burn quickly!* They should be soft and pliable, not crispy, with a hint of bitterness, which remains even after cooking.

Serve soup in bowls garnished with tortilla and chile strips, avocado slices, and *queso fresco*.

SOPA DE MILPA

This soup honors the milpa, the sustainable crop-growing system throughout Mesoamerica. More than just a system of agriculture, it is a worldview that honors the connection between farmers, crops, land, and cosmos. Our soup features the life-affirming flavors of the summer garden, from blossom to tender squash to mature corn and chiles.

....

Prepare squash blossoms: If there is a long pistil in center of blossom, remove and discard. Rinse flowers gently under cool water. Gently tear squash blossoms in half.

Prepare poblanos: Read directions on p. 53 for roasting chiles. Tear chiles into strips about ¼-in (6-mm) wide and cut each strip 3–4 in (8–10 cm) long.

In a large saucepan on medium heat, sauté onions in oil about 10 minutes, until golden brown. Add garlic and stir until fragrance is released, about 30 seconds. Add corn stock, chiles, zucchini, corn, and epazote and bring to a light boil. Simmer for 20 minutes. Add squash blossom pieces and cook for 5–10 minutes, or until zucchini is crisp-tender. Add salt and pepper. Taste and adjust seasonings. Ladle soup into bowls and serve topped with avocado cubes and *queso fresco.*

15 squash blossoms

2 fresh poblano chiles, roasted, peeled, and seeded

½ medium white onion, finely chopped

1 tbsp olive oil

2 garlic cloves, peeled and finely diced

6 cups (1 ½ L) corn stock (p. 90)

2 medium zucchinis, sliced into bite-sized quarter-rounds

2–3 ears of corn, to make 2 cups (500 mL) kernels

2 tbsp chopped fresh epazote or cilantro

½ tsp sea salt

⅛ tsp white pepper

2 avocados, peeled, seeded, and cubed

6 oz (175 g) queso fresco, cubed (optional)

GARDENER'S NOTE:

What's growing in your garden? Because this soup celebrates the land used to grow food, feel free to add a vegetable that you have grown yourself! This recipe features crops that are harvested in late summer or early fall. Fresh green beans, nopales, carrots, chayote, verdolagas, or seasonal mushrooms would be wonderful additions or substitutions.

makes 6 servings

NEW MEXICO GREEN CHILE STEW

1 large onion, chopped

1 tbsp extra virgin coconut oil

3 large garlic cloves, peeled and minced

3 large red tomatoes, diced

¼ tsp sea salt

4 cups (1 L) vegetable stock

1 tsp dried oregano, preferably Mexican

6 medium red potatoes, diced

1–2 cups (250–500 mL) roasted, peeled, and chopped New Mexico (or Anaheim or poblano) mild–medium green chiles (about 3–6 chiles)

¾ tsp sea salt

¼ tsp white pepper

3 medium zucchinis, diced

This is the first meal that Catriona cooked for Luz and is a vegan version of New Mexico stew. You can eat it alone, with a side of tortillas and beans, or you can use it as a sauce to smother a bean burrito, another classic New Mexican dish.

....

In a heavy pot on medium-high heat, sauté onions in oil until just starting to brown. Add garlic and stir until fragrance is released, about 30 seconds. Add tomatoes and ¼ tsp salt. Cook until tomatoes release their juice, about 3–4 minutes. Add stock, oregano, potatoes, 1 cup (250 mL) green chiles, salt, and pepper. Bring to a boil then reduce heat to medium low. Simmer for 30 minutes or until potatoes are almost tender. Add zucchinis and cook until they are crisp-tender, about 15 minutes.

For a thicker stew, blend 1 cup (250 mL) vegetables from stew in a blender and return to pot. Taste stew and adjust seasonings, adding remainder of chiles as desired.

TORTILLA SOUP

This flavorful, nutritious soup brings together the rich flavors of Mesoamerican cuisine: dried chiles, corn tortillas, summer squash, and fresh corn. Use this recipe as a base for your own creativity: vary vegetables or add greens, but keep the core components: crispy slivers of tortillas and a chile-tomato broth enlivened by fresh lime juice.

....

Preheat oven to 450° F (230° C). Place onions, tomatoes, and unpeeled garlic in a baking dish. Toss with olive oil, oregano and salt. Roast for 45 minutes, tossing every 15 minutes. Onions and tomatoes should be black around the edges. Lower oven temperature to 400°F (200°C) before baking tortilla strips.

On a dry griddle on medium heat, toast—but do not burn—dried chiles for 1 minute on each side. Put chiles in a bowl and cover with boiling water. Use a small plate to keep chiles submerged for 30 minutes. Drain chiles, reserving soaking liquid. Remove stems and seeds and put chiles in blender with 1 cup (250 mL) soaking liquid. Blend until smooth. Peel roasted garlic. Add garlic, onions, tomatoes, and roasting juices into blender with chile. Add 2 cups (500 mL) water, blend until smooth, then pass blended mixture through a medium sieve into a large pot. Press on solids to extract as much liquid as possible, then discard. Straining makes for a thin, bright, flavorful broth. Season with salt and pepper. Add 4 more cups (1 L) water to broth, and bring to a simmer. Cover, reduce heat to medium-low, and simmer gently for 10 minutes. Add zucchinis, corn, cilantro, salt, and pepper and continue to simmer for another 10 minutes, or until zucchini is crisp-tender.

- 1 large white onion, peeled and quartered
- 4 large ripe red tomatoes, cored and quartered
- 4 unpeeled garlic cloves
- 2 tbsp olive oil
- 1 tsp dried oregano, preferably Mexican
- ¼ tsp sea salt
- 2 dried guajillo chiles
- 1 dried pasilla chile
- 1 tsp sea salt
- ¼ tsp white pepper
- 3 medium zucchinis, diced
- 2–3 ears of corn, to make 2 cups (500 mL) kernels (fresh if in season, otherwise frozen)
- 1 bunch cilantro, including stems, chopped (reserve 2 tbsp leaves for garnish)
- sea salt and freshly ground black pepper, to taste

CONTINUED ▶

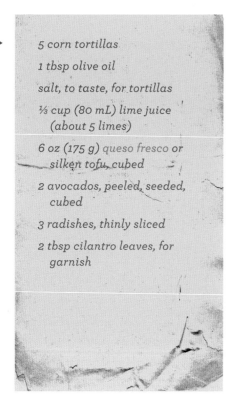

5 corn tortillas

1 tbsp olive oil

salt, to taste, for tortillas

⅓ cup (80 mL) lime juice (about 5 limes)

6 oz (175 g) *queso fresco* or silken tofu, cubed

2 avocados, peeled, seeded, cubed

3 radishes, thinly sliced

2 tbsp cilantro leaves, for garnish

To make tortilla strips: Preheat oven to 400°F (200°C). Cut tortillas in half, then crosswise into ¼-in (6-mm) strips. Add tortilla strips to a mixing bowl. Slowly drizzle in olive oil while tossing strips. Sprinkle salt on tortillas and toss to combine. Spread strips over a cookie sheet and bake for 15 minutes, turning strips after 8 minutes. Set aside.

Add lime juice to soup just before serving. To serve, place 2–3 cubes *queso fresco* or tofu in each bowl. Ladle hot soup into bowls and garnish with a generous scoop of avocado cubes, a heap of tortilla strips, several radish slices, and some cilantro leaves.

ABUELITAS' LENTIL SOUP

Lentils are not indigenous to the Americas, but both of our grandmothers (abuelitas) made delicious and soul-warming sopa de lentejas. We flavor our soup with yerbaníz (also called "grandmother plant"), which has many medicinal properties, including being good for respiratory conditions and soothing to the stomach. The final squeeze of lemon sends the iron from the lentils to your body and adds brightness to the flavor.

....

In a large pot on medium high heat, sauté onions in oil until lightly browned, about 7–8 minutes. Add jalapeño, carrots, and chard stems and cook for 5 minutes, until vegetables soften. Add garlic and freshly ground pepper and cook for 1 minute. Add stock, lentils, and *yerbaníz*. Bring mixture to a slow boil. Reduce heat, and cook at a slow simmer until lentils are barely tender, about 25 minutes. Add salt, chard leaves, and cilantro and cook, stirring occasionally, until wilted, about 3 minutes. Add ground chia seeds, cover partially, and continue to simmer for 10 more minutes. Stir in lemon juice. Taste and adjust seasonings, adding more salt, pepper, or lemon juice until soup has a nice balance of flavors.

1 large onion, finely chopped

3 tbsp olive oil

2–3 jalapeños, diced

1 carrot, diced

1 bunch green Swiss chard, stems diced, leaves cut into thin ribbons

4 garlic cloves, finely chopped

freshly ground black pepper, to taste

8 cups (2 L) vegetable stock or water

2 cups (500 mL) brown lentils, rinsed

2 tbsp chopped fresh yerbaníz or 1 tbsp dried yerbaníz or 2 tsp dried French tarragon

2 tsp sea salt

1 bunch cilantro, chopped

1 tbsp chia seeds, ground (optional)

juice of 1–2 lemons, to taste

RED POZOLE WITH MEDICINAL MUSHROOMS

Pozole (pozolli in Nahuatl) celebrates the flavor of nixtamal, or hominy. Our recipe is inspired by a Native American cuisine workshop given by chefs Lois Ellen Frank (Kiowa), and Walter Whitewater (Diné). For the first course of their spectacular meal, they served a vegan pozole seasoned with tomatoes, chile, and Mexican saffron. We replicate the spirit of their pozole here, adding dried maitake mushrooms to lend a unique textural (and healing) element. Note: if using dried hominy, first soak in water overnight.

....

If using dried hominy: Drain and rinse soaked hominy. In a large pot on high heat, add hominy with enough unsalted water to cover. Add peeled garlic and bring to a boil. Reduce heat to medium-low and cook for 3–5 hours, or until hominy is tender and corn kernels have opened up or "bloomed." Check often and add water as needed. When hominy has bloomed, add 1 tsp salt and cook for 30 minutes. Remove from heat and set aside.

Clean dried chiles with a wet cloth. Heat a griddle on medium and toast—do not burn—chiles, 1 minute per side. Place chiles in a heatproof bowl. Place mushrooms in another heatproof bowl. Pour boiling water over chiles and mushrooms, to cover, and let soak for 30 minutes. Drain chiles, and remove stems and seeds. Place chiles in blender. Reserving soaking liquid, drain mushrooms, rinse very well to remove grit, and set aside. Using a griddle on high heat, toast unpeeled garlic and tomatoes until they begin to char. Remove peel from garlic, and put garlic and tomatoes in blender. Add 2 cups (500 mL) water and blend until very smooth, at least 1 minute.

½ lb (250 g) dried hominy or 4 cups (1 L) canned

5 garlic cloves, if using dried hominy, peeled and crushed

1 tsp salt

3 dried red New Mexico chiles

1 dried chile de árbol

1 oz (30 g) dried maitake mushrooms

3 whole, unpeeled garlic cloves

2 plum tomatoes

1 white onion, chopped

1 tsp safflower (also called Mexican saffron or azafrán)

2 tbsp olive oil

2 bay leaves

1 tbsp dried oregano, preferably Mexican, for garnish

1 tsp dried thyme

1 tsp sea salt

¼ tsp white pepper

1 bunch cilantro, stems removed, chopped, for garnish

4 watermelon radishes, very thinly sliced, for garnish

½ green cabbage, sliced into very thin ribbons, for garnish

3 tbsp dried oregano, preferably Mexican, for garnish

3 limes, quartered, for garnish

Sopas y Guisados: Soups & Stews • 101

▶▶ In a large pot on medium heat, sauté onions and safflower in oil for 7 minutes. Add bay leaves, oregano, and thyme and stir to combine until aroma of bay leaves is released, about 1 minute. With a medium sieve, strain contents of blender into pot. Add salt and pepper. Add 2 cups (500 mL) water and bring mixture to a boil. Reduce heat to low, cover, and simmer for 20 minutes.

Tear soaked mushrooms into bite-sized pieces. Filter mushroom soaking liquid through a coffee filter. Add mushrooms, 1 cup (250 mL) mushroom soaking liquid, and drained hominy to pot. Add more water if stew is too thick. Simmer on medium heat for 20 minutes to meld flavors and cook mushrooms. Taste and adjust seasonings. Ladle into bowls and allow guests to garnish with cilantro, radishes, cabbage, oregano, and a squeeze of lime.

▶

HISTORICAL NOTE:

In her discussion of atolli *(atole) among the ancient Maya in America's First Cuisines, Sophie Coe writes, "Of course,* atolli *could be varied by adding other ingredients … Chile was indispensable, but there were also beans, floated with their broth on top of the* atolli *and ground toasted squash seeds to mix in. The marigold species, Tagetes lucida, (yerbaníz, in this recipe) which is said to smell like cinnamon, could be added."*

HEALING GREEN CHILEATOLE

Atole, from the word atolli *in Nahuatl, is a hot corn-based beverage. There are dozens of different atole preparations—sweet, bitter, savory, and spicy. More a soup than a drink, we find this spicy chileatole to be both healing and energizing. Full of powerful herbs, it is the perfect food when you are feeling worn down.*

....

Preheat to 425°F (220°C).

Roughly chop ½ onion. Dice the other half and set aside. In a glass baking dish, toss chopped onions, tomatillos, and unpeeled garlic in olive oil. Roast for 15 minutes. Allow to cool slightly and remove garlic skins by snipping stem end and squeezing out roasted cloves.

Place fresh masa or masa harina in a blender with 2 cups (500 mL) corn stock and process until smooth. Add roasted tomatillos, onions, and garlic and blend thoroughly. Add epazote, *yerbaníz*, and chives, and blend thoroughly. Add jalapeños, ½ at a time, blending after each addition and checking for taste. Chileatole should be on the spicy side. Continue to add chiles until desired level of spiciness is obtained. Add more water as necessary to get a smooth consistency. Through a medium sieve, strain purée into remainder of corn stock. Pour into a pot and heat gently on medium-low, stirring often. Do not allow mixture to come to boil. This stock thickens with cooking so keep a close eye on it.

Meanwhile, in a frying pan on medium heat, melt coconut oil. Sauté corn, diced onions, and zucchinis for about 4 minutes. Add sautéed vegetables and salt to soup, and cook on medium heat for 4–5 minutes, or until zucchini is crisp-tender. Stir in cilantro. Taste and adjust seasonings, adding more salt if necessary. Ladle soup into bowls. Add 1 tsp lime juice to each bowl.

1 white onion, peeled and halved

2 large tomatillos, husks removed, rinsed

3 garlic cloves

1 tsp olive oil

½ cup (125 mL) fresh masa for tortillas or ½ cup (125 mL) masa harina

4 cups (1 L) corn stock or corn silk tea (p. 90)

5 fresh epazote or parsley sprigs or 1 tbsp dried

¼ cup (60 mL) yerbaníz leaves, loosely packed (optional)

¼ cup (60mL) chopped chives

1–3 jalapeño or serrano chiles, cut in half, stems removed

1 tbsp extra virgin coconut oil

about 2 ears of corn, to make 1 ½ cups (375 mL) kernels (fresh if in season, otherwise frozen)

1 medium zucchini, diced

¾ tsp sea salt

1 cup (250 mL) finely chopped cilantro, loosely packed

4 tsp lime juice

VERDOLAGAS, BEANS & BUTTERNUT SQUASH STEW

makes 4 servings

This hearty stew is a wonderful way to enjoy the health benefits of verdolagas. The tomatillos and the purslane are both tart, the chiles give the dish some heat, and the squash and beans provide substance. Serve with corn tortillas.

....

Preheat oven to 425°F (220°C).

In a glass baking dish, toss tomatillos, onions, and garlic in oil and roast for 15 minutes, turning once to roast evenly. Allow garlic to cool, then snip ends and squeeze out roasted cloves. In a blender, purée tomatillos, onions, and garlic with cumin, 1 chile, 4 cups (1 L) water, cilantro, masa harina, salt, and pepper. Dice remainder of chiles and set aside.

In a large saucepan on medium-high, heat oil. Add tomatillo mixture and bring to a slow boil. Stir in squash, oregano, and diced chiles and reduce heat to medium. Simmer until squash is tender, about 20 minutes. Add purslane and beans and cook about 5 minutes, until purslane is wilted and beans are heated through. Stir in lime juice and adjust seasonings. Serve in bowls, topped with slices of avocado and cilantro sprigs.

COOK'S NOTE:
Green chiles vary a lot when it comes to heat. If chiles are spicy and a milder stew is desired, use fewer chiles. Taste the chiles before you add them, so you know how spicy they are. Let your taste buds be the guide!

½ lb (250 g) tomatillos, husked and rinsed (about 5)

1 white onion, chopped

3 large, unpeeled garlic cloves

1 tsp olive oil

1 tsp cumin seeds, toasted and ground

5 fresh Anaheim green chiles, roasted, seeded, and peeled

½ bunch cilantro

1 tbsp masa harina

1 tsp sea salt

½ tsp pepper

1 tbsp extra virgin coconut oil

2 lb (900 g) butternut squash, peeled and diced

1 tsp dried oregano, preferably Mexican

1 cup (250 mL) purslane, including stems, cut into 2-in (5-cm) pieces

2 cups (500 mL) cooked white beans or 1 15-oz (425-g) can

3 tbsp lime juice

2 avocados, peeled, seeded, and sliced

4 cilantro sprigs

CALDO DE QUINOA

This soup has been in our regular dinner rotation for more than 15 years. A warming comfort food that never grows old, filled with different vegetables and quinoa, it provides powerful nourishment. Take this soup to a friend who needs a gentle meal to heal the body and spirit.

....

Rinse quinoa in a bowl of cold water and strain through a fine sieve. In a saucepan on medium heat, melt coconut oil. Add wet quinoa and toast until dry, about 3–4 minutes. Add 2 cups (500 mL) water and ½ tsp salt. Increase heat to high and bring mixture to a boil. Cover and reduce heat to low. Cook for 20 minutes. Remove from heat, uncover, and fluff with a fork. Set aside.

In a large sturdy pot on medium-high heat, sauté onions until soft, about 5 minutes. Add bell peppers and carrots and continue to cook for 10 minutes. Add tomatoes, jalapeño, garlic, cumin, coriander, oregano, salt, and pepper. Stir quickly to coat vegetables in spices. Continue to cook until tomato releases its juices, about 5 minutes.

Add vegetable stock and bring mixture to a slow boil. Reduce heat to low, cover, and simmer for 15 minutes. Add squash and continue to cook until squash are crisp-tender, about 10 minutes. Stir in cooked quinoa and cilantro. Add lime juice and adjust seasonings. If soup is too thick, add water as needed. (We like ours to be quite thick!) Serve soup in bowls, topped with cubes of avocado and *queso fresco*. Garnish with a few cilantro leaves.

---

1 cup (250 mL) quinoa

1 tsp extra virgin coconut oil, for toasting quinoa

½ tsp sea salt, for seasoning quinoa

2 tsp extra virgin coconut oil, for sautéing vegetables

1 white onion, diced

1 yellow or red bell pepper, seeded and diced

2 carrots, scrubbed and cut into half or quarter moons

1 large tomato, diced

1 fresh jalapeño, minced

4 garlic cloves, minced

2 tsp cumin seeds, toasted and ground

1 tsp coriander seeds, toasted and ground

1 tsp dried oregano

½ tsp sea salt

¼ tsp white pepper

4 cups (1 L) vegetable stock or water

3–4 medium summer squash (zucchini or patty pans) cut into half or quarter moons

1 bunch cilantro, chopped (reserve 20 leaves for garnish)

2 tbsp lime juice

sea salt, to taste

2 avocados, peeled, seeded, and cubed

½ cup (125 mL) cubed queso fresco

CHAYA SOUP WITH ZUCCHINI, MINT & CHILE

This green puréed soup is garnished with edible blossoms. Chaya, or "tree spinach," a traditional ingredient in Mayan cuisine, is rich in potassium, calcium, antioxidants, and healing phytochemicals. When cooking chaya, always use a non-reactive pot made of ceramic, glass, or stainless steel (cooking this soup in aluminum may release a toxic chemical). Serve and eat immediately to preserve the vibrant color of the soup. (Adapted from Deborah Madison's Local Flavors: Cooking and Eating from America's Farmers' Markets).

....

In a covered, non-reactive pot, simmer chaya leaves in 4 cups (1 L) water for 20 minutes.

Meanwhile, in a dry griddle on medium-high heat, toast pumpkin seeds until they start to puff up or turn brown, about 3 minutes. Toss them with salt and set aside. Reduce heat to low and toast corn tortilla on griddle until crisp and a bit charred, about 5 minutes per side. Break tortilla into several pieces and set aside.

In a large pot on medium heat, sauté onions in oil until translucent, about 5 minutes. Add chile, ¼ bunch cilantro, zucchinis, mint, and salt. Cook, stirring occasionally, for 5 minutes. Add chaya with cooking liquid and tortilla pieces. Increase heat and bring soup to a slow boil, then reduce heat to low. Partially cover, and simmer soup until zucchini is soft, about 15 minutes. Add remainder of cilantro. Use an immersion blender to purée soup until completely smooth. If soup is too thick, add more water. Add lime juice and several grinds of black pepper. Taste and adjust seasoning. Garnish each serving with an edible flower, toasted pumpkin seeds, and a drizzle of pumpkin seed oil.

15 fresh chaya leaves

½ cup (125 mL) raw, hulled pumpkin seeds

salt, to taste, for pumpkin seeds

1 corn tortilla

1 white onion, peeled and chopped

1 tbsp extra virgin coconut oil

1 fresh poblano chile, roasted, seeded, peeled, and torn in strips

1 bunch cilantro

3–4 medium zucchinis, chopped

20 mint leaves

1 tsp sea salt

1 tbsp lime juice

freshly ground pepper, to taste

4 edible flowers, such as borage, chive, or nasturtium

1 tbsp pumpkin seed oil

CONTINUED ▶

▶▶ *If fresh chaya is not available, substitute 6 dried chaya leaves (Lucia's Herbal Remedies at* mexgrocer.com *sells dried chaya leaves as a tea) and 2 cups (500 mL) lightly packed fresh spinach. Place dried chaya leaves in 4 cups (1 L) water, bring to a boil, reduce heat to low, and simmer for 20 minutes. Strain out dried chaya and use this "tea" as stock for soup. Add spinach at the same time that recipe calls for zucchini.*

TIP:

An immersion blender is a handy and relatively inexpensive tool that is useful for making creamy soups without dairy. If an immersion blender is not available, use a regular blender, remembering to be careful when working around hot liquids! Allow soup to cool slightly. Working in batches, pour a small amount of soup into blender. Cover blender lid with a folded dishtowel and hold in place. Pulse once and open blender to allow steam to escape. Repeat this process twice and then begin to blend, starting on low and building up to high speed.

CHAPTER SIX
Platos Fuertes: Main Dishes

▶

HEALTH NOTES:

These spices don't just make your dishes taste good, they have multiple health benefits as well.

- ALLSPICE: *Rich in natural compounds called polyphenols. Research suggests that these compounds may help prevent cancer.*

- CAYENNE AND OTHER CHILES: *Boost immunity, clear congestion, and have cardiovascular benefits.*

- CORIANDER: *Good for stabilizing glucose levels, is anti-inflammatory, and may lower cholesterol.*

- CUMIN: *High in iron, good for digestion, and has anti-cancer properties.*

- OREGANO: *Contains the antibacterial volatile oils thymol and carvacrol. It is also very high in cancer-fighting antioxidants.*

CHICANA POWER CHILI BEANS

Activists in the middle of campaigns too often subsist on pizza and fast food. We believe that taking better care of each other (and ourselves) is critical to the success of activism over the long term. This dish provides substance, packs nutrition, and is always quickly devoured by hungry organizers! In one study, small red beans were found to have more antioxidants than blueberries, which motivated Luz to develop this recipe as a tasty way to eat more small red beans. Serve with Skillet Cornbread (p. 161) and a green salad for a full meal.

....

In a small frying pan on medium heat, sauté onions in oil until completely soft and almost translucent, about 10 minutes. Add garlic, cumin, coriander, allspice, oregano, ancho, cayenne, and paprika, and stir gently until fragrant, about 30 seconds. Put beans, onion mixture, tomatoes, and stock in slow cooker and cook on high heat for 4–6 hours or low heat 6–9 hours. Watch water level; if beans begin to dry out, add more water. When beans are almost done, add salt and adjust seasonings. If chili is not spicy enough, add more cayenne pepper ½ tsp at a time, to taste. Serve chili beans topped with cilantro, avocado slices, green onions, and grated cheese.

1 onion, peeled and chopped

1 tbsp olive oil

3 garlic cloves, peeled and minced

1 tsp cumin seeds, toasted and ground

1 tsp coriander seeds, toasted and ground

4 allspice berries, toasted and ground

2 tsp dried oregano, preferably Mexican

2 tsp ground ancho chile

½ tsp cayenne pepper

2 tbsp smoked paprika

1 cup (250 mL) dried pinto beans, rinsed and sorted

1 cup (250 mL) dried small red beans, rinsed and sorted

1 cup (250 mL) dried black beans, rinsed and sorted

1 14.5-oz (411-g) can chopped organic tomatoes (or 5 fresh tomatoes chopped)

8 cups (2 L) vegetable stock or water

1 tbsp sea salt

1 bunch cilantro, chopped

1 avocado, peeled, pitted, and sliced

1 bunch green onions, diced

6 oz (175 g) jack or cheddar cheese, grated (optional)

PORTOBELLO FAJITAS

3 garlic cloves, peeled

1 tsp cumin seeds, toasted and ground

1 tsp coriander seeds, toasted and ground

2 tbsp olive oil

4 tbsp lime juice

1 jalapeño, minced

1 tsp dried oregano, preferably Mexican

½ tsp sea salt

⅛ tsp white pepper

3 large portobello mushrooms, stems removed

1 orange bell pepper, stems and seeds removed

1 medium white onion, diced

2 tbsp olive oil

1 large red tomato, finely diced

1 tbsp tomato paste

This dish is inspired by our friend Maylei Blackwell, who served it to us one night in her small cottage in the Beach Flats in Santa Cruz. She was improvising a vegetarian version of Texas-style fajitas. The portobello mushrooms have a rich meatiness, and marinating them really adds to the flavor. Serve with Borderlands Whole Wheat Tortillas (p. 160), Classic Guacamole (p. 68), and Roasted Guajillo Salsa (p. 170).

....

In a mortar and pestle, mash garlic with cumin and coriander to form a paste. In a small bowl, combine paste with oil, lime juice, jalapeño, oregano, salt, and pepper, and whisk together. Slice mushrooms, bell peppers, and onions into ½-in (1-cm) thick strips. In a salad bowl, toss mushrooms, bell peppers, and onions with marinade, and let sit for 15–30 minutes, tossing occasionally.

In a large frying pan on medium, heat olive oil. Pour in marinated vegetables. Add diced tomatoes. Cover and cook for about 15 minutes, stirring occasionally. Add tomato paste to create a thick sauce. Lower heat, and continue to cook for 10 minutes. Taste and adjust seasonings.

COYOLXAUHQUI BOWL

Chicana feminists have reclaimed Coyolxauhqui, a Mexica goddess figure, seeing in her a rebellious daughter who resists patriarchy. We intend this dish to provide sustenance to women, gender non-conforming people, and male allies as we heal ourselves from the violence of colonization and patriarchy.

....

In a frying pan with a tight-fighting lid, heat oil on medium-high until hot. Reduce heat to low, add garlic, and swirl to release aroma, about 15 seconds. Stir in onions, nopales, chile, cilantro, and salt. Cover and cook for about 10 minutes or until nopales are tender. At this point, nopales should have released their gel and mixture should be extremely juicy. Remove lid and continue to cook until all liquid evaporates, up to 20 minutes. If it takes longer, increase heat and stir constantly to prevent burning. Remove from heat when no liquid remains.

In a saucepan on medium heat, warm beans. Divide brown rice evenly between 6 serving bowls then add ½ cup (125 mL) beans. Top with a generous scoop of nopales, drizzle salsa in a spiral around bowl, and garnish with cilantro sprigs.

2 tbsp extra virgin coconut oil

2 garlic cloves, chopped

½ white onion, thinly sliced

6 nopal paddles, cleaned, spines removed, and diced

1 fresh jalapeño, minced

¼ cup chopped cilantro

1 tsp sea salt

3 cups (750 mL) Old School Pinto Beans, served whole not mashed (p. 151)

2 cups (500 mL) cooked brown rice

Raw Green Salsa (p. 174)

6 cilantro sprigs

RED PIPIAN OVER RICE

Pipian is a traditional Mayan dish with a sauce made of dried chiles and pumpkin seeds. The rich color reminds us of beautiful terracotta clay. In our vegan version, we incorporate hearty vegetables indigenous to the Americas: potatoes, green beans, and chayote. This stew is even better the second day. Serve in bowls over a bed of rice with Pachamama Green Salad (p. 78) and Corn Tortillas (p. 155).

....

To make sauce:

On a griddle on medium-high heat, toast corn tortillas until crispy and slightly charred. Set aside. On same griddle, toast dried chiles for 1 minute on each side, taking care not to burn. Put chiles in a bowl and cover with boiling water. Use a small plate to keep chiles submerged for 30 minutes.

On same hot griddle, slightly char onions and garlic, about 4 minutes. Peel garlic and place it with onions in blender. Put whole tomatoes on griddle and turn often to char on several sides, then add to blender. When chiles have finished soaking, remove stems, veins, and seeds and add to blender. On same hot griddle, toast pumpkin seeds until they begin to puff up. Reserve ¼ cup (60 mL) pumpkin seeds for garnish, and add the rest to blender. On griddle, toast allspice and peppercorns for a few seconds and add to blender with achiote, salt, and pepper. Break charred tortillas into quarters and add to blender. Purée until ingredients form a smooth sauce. If necessary, work in batches or add a small amount of water to blender to process smoothly. Sauce should have consistency of a tomato sauce or just a little bit chunkier.

Sauce:

2 corn tortillas

3 dried guajillo chiles

5 dried pasilla chiles

1 dried chile de árbol

1 white onion, peeled and quartered

2 whole, unpeeled garlic cloves

2 medium tomatoes

¾ cup (175 mL) raw, hulled pumpkin seeds

8 whole allspice berries

6 peppercorns

1 tsp ground achiote

½ tsp sea salt

¼ tsp pepper

CONTINUED ▶

▶▶ *Stew:*

*5 medium-sized purple
   potatoes, scrubbed*

*½ lb (250 g) green beans, ends
   removed*

1 chayote, peeled

1 onion, diced

3 tbsp olive oil

4 garlic cloves, minced

½ tsp sea salt

2 tbsp pumpkin seed oil

*2 cups (500 mL) cooked rice
   (white or brown)*

*¼ cup (60 mL) raw, hulled
   pumpkin seeds, for garnish*

*¼ cup (60 mL) cilantro, leaves
   only*

To make stew:

Coarsely chop potatoes, green beans, and chayote into hearty, bite-sized chunks and set aside. In a large pot on medium heat, sauté onions in olive oil for 5 minutes. Add garlic and stir until fragrant. Add potatoes, green beans, and chayote and stir to combine. Season vegetables with salt. Add just enough water to cover vegetables and bring to a boil. Stir in pipian sauce. Lower heat to medium and simmer, stirring occasionally, for about 30 minutes or until vegetables are fork-tender. Adjust seasonings. Divide rice between bowls and serve pipian over rice. Garnish each serving with a drizzle of pumpkin seed oil, pumpkin seeds, and cilantro leaves.

CHILES RELLENOS REMIX

makes 4 servings

Chiles rellenos (literally "stuffed chiles") are commonly prepared with an egg batter, deep fried, and stuffed with jack cheese. In this lighter version, we stuff the roasted green chiles with a quinoa, corn, and pine nut pilaf and serve them in a bath of roasted tomatillo sauce. This dish is best made in late summer, when poblano chiles and corn are being harvested.

....

Preheat oven to 375°F (190°C).

Rinse quinoa in a bowl of cold water and strain through a fine sieve. In a frying pan on medium heat, melt 1 tsp coconut oil. Add wet quinoa and toast until dry, about 3 minutes. Add 2 cups (500 mL) water and ½ tsp salt. Increase heat to high and bring mixture to a boil. Cover and reduce heat to low. Cook for 15 minutes, remove from heat, and allow mixture to rest for 5 minutes. Uncover and fluff with a fork.

In a small frying pan on medium heat, melt 1 tsp coconut oil. Add onions and bell peppers and sauté until soft, about 5 minutes. Add corn, ½ tsp salt, pepper, cumin, and oregano and cook for 3 minutes. In a mixing bowl, combine quinoa, cilantro, and sautéed vegetables.

In a hot, dry frying pan on medium heat, toast pine nuts for 3–4 minutes. Add half to quinoa mixture, reserving remainder for garnish. Stir to combine and adjust seasonings, if necessary.

Carefully cut a slit in poblano chiles and remove seeds. Arrange slit side up in a greased baking dish. Using a spoon, carefully stuff quinoa filling into chiles. Top each with goat cheese. Sprinkle with remainder of pine nuts. Bake for 15 minutes.

In a saucepan on medium heat, warm up sauce. Serve chiles rellenos in shallow bowls on top of ½ cup (125 mL) Classic Green Tomatillo Sauce.

---

1 cup (250 mL) quinoa

1 tsp extra virgin coconut oil

½ tsp sea salt

1 tsp extra virgin coconut oil

½ small red onion, minced

½ red bell pepper, minced

1 ear of corn, to make ¾ cup (175 mL) kernels (fresh if in season, otherwise frozen)

½ tsp sea salt

⅛ tsp pepper

½ tsp cumin seeds, toasted and ground

1 tsp dried oregano, preferably Mexican

¼ cup (60 mL) chopped cilantro

½ cup (125 mL) shelled pine nuts or raw shelled sunflower seeds

8 fresh poblano chiles, roasted and carefully peeled, leaving stem intact

5 oz (150 g) fresh goat cheese or ½ cup (125 mL) Cashew Crema (p. 183) (optional)

2 cups (500 mL) Classic Green Tomatillo Sauce (p. 176)

RED ENCHILADAS STUFFED WITH POTATOES, GREENS & PUMPKIN SEEDS

4 cups (1 L) firmly packed quelites (lamb's quarters) leaves or 1 bunch Lacinato kale

1 tbsp extra virgin coconut oil

1 white onion, diced

½ tsp sea salt

2 medium red potatoes, diced

¾ tsp sea salt

⅛ tsp pepper

½ tsp apple cider vinegar

½ cup (125 mL) pumpkin seeds

¼ tsp sea salt

about 4 cups (1 L) Classic Red Chile Sauce (p. 175)

¼ tsp extra virgin coconut oil

18–22 corn tortillas

1 Pickled Red Onion (p. 180), for garnish

¼ cup (60 mL) cilantro leaves, for garnish

½ cup (125 mL) Cashew Crema (p. 183) or 6 oz (175 g) crumbled queso cotija, for garnish

Real enchiladas—with a homemade sauce and fresh fillings—are rich, tasty, and healthy. This dish was inspired by a pan of enchiladas served to us by our friend Yvonne Yarbro-Bejarano one foggy night in San Francisco. We loved the combination of velvety potatoes, bitter kale, and rich pumpkin seeds. Be creative and try new combinations for fillings: roasted winter squash and caramelized onions, sweet potatoes and Swiss chard, or hibiscus flowers and grated jícama are all delicious.

....

Preheat oven to 350°F (180°C).

If using *quelites*, use only the leaves, which can be left whole. If using kale, remove fibrous ribs and stems and chop kale into small pieces.

In a large frying pan on medium heat, melt 1 tbsp coconut oil. Add onions, and sauté until translucent, about 10 minutes. Add greens, ½ tsp salt, and ½ cup (125 mL) water. Cover and cook until greens are tender, about 10 minutes. Remove cover and allow remainder of water to evaporate. Remove from heat.

In a medium pot on high heat, parboil potatoes in boiling water for 5 minutes. Drain and transfer with greens mixture to a small mixing bowl. Season with salt, pepper, and apple cider vinegar.

In a hot, dry frying pan, toast pumpkin seeds until they start to puff up or turn brown, about 3 minutes. Remove pan from heat and toss with ¼ tsp salt. Reserve half for garnish. Finely chop remainder and stir into potato/greens mixture.

To assemble enchiladas:

Put about ½ cup (125 mL) red sauce in 2 10 x 15-in casseroles (4 L each). Rub ¼ tsp coconut oil on hot cast-iron griddle and heat tortillas one by one, flipping to heat thoroughly on both sides. Warmed tortillas should be soft and pliable—don't toast. Add more oil, as needed, after every couple of tortillas.

This method replaces "frying" the tortilla. Place tortilla in sauce in baking pan and flip over, coating both sides. Place 1 heaping tbsp greens/potato mixture on tortilla and roll up. Scoot enchilada to edge of pan. Repeat with remainder of tortillas and stuffing. Add more sauce to baking pan and continue until pans are full of enchiladas sitting in a row (about 9–10 enchiladas per pan). Add more sauce as necessary. Once pan is almost full, assemble last enchiladas on a dinner plate and transfer to pan. When completed, spoon remainder of sauce on top of enchiladas. Cover baking pans with foil and bake for 20 minutes. Serve enchiladas garnished with Pickled Red Onions, cilantro leaves, and *queso cotija* or Cashew Crema.

SLOW-COOKER STACKED ENCHILADAS

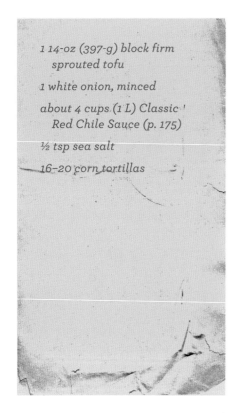

1 14-oz (397-g) block firm
   sprouted tofu

1 white onion, minced

about 4 cups (1 L) Classic
   Red Chile Sauce (p. 175)

½ tsp sea salt

16–20 corn tortillas

In New Mexico, enchiladas are stacked instead of rolled. Catriona developed this vegan dish to be cooked in a slow cooker. Steaming the tortillas with the sauce produces something akin to a corn and chile pudding. Great for potlucks or cold winter nights served with a crisp green salad.

....

Grate tofu on coarse side of a box grater and combine with minced onions, ½ cup (125 mL) Classic Red Chile Sauce and salt.

On a griddle on medium-high, heat tortillas gently until soft and pliable.

Pour ½ cup (125 mL) Classic Red Chile Sauce into slow cooker then cover with tortilla. Add a scant ¼ cup (60 mL) sauce, and a scant ¼ cup (60 mL) tofu mixture. Repeat these layers—sauce, tortilla, tofu mixture—until slow cooker is three-quarters full. Finish with a corn tortilla and pour remainder of sauce over top. Cover and cook on high heat until slow cooker gets steamy, 20–60 minutes. Reduce heat to low and cook for 2–3 hours. (Or just cook on low for 3–5 hours.) Slice enchiladas like a pie into 8 slices.

CHILAQUILES WITH BEAN SAUCE

Instead of being smothered in a traditional red or green chile sauce, these chilaquiles are enveloped in a fragrant black bean sauce flavored with avocado leaf and epazote. They use healthy, oven-crisped corn tortillas and the garnishes add a fresh note.

....

Rinse and sort beans. Put in a slow cooker along with onions, garlic, cumin, epazote, and avocado leaves. Add 3 cups (750 mL) water and cook on high heat for 4–6 hours or low heat 6–9 hours. When beans begin to soften, add salt. When beans are done, use an immersion blender to purée into a smooth sauce.

Preheat oven to 400°F (200°C).

Place tortillas on 2 cookie sheets, overlapping as little as possible. Bake for 17 minutes, turning tortillas over at the halfway point. Remove from oven and cool. Break each tortilla into 6 irregular pieces.

Reduce oven heat to 350°F (180°C). Spoon about ½ cup (125 mL) bean purée in casserole dish. Add a layer of tortilla pieces. Repeat until all tortillas are used. Cover in remainder of sauce. Cover with foil and bake for 25 minutes. Garnish with cheese or Cashew Crema, Pickled Red Onions, hot sauce, avocado slices, and cilantro sprigs.

Along with epazote, Mexican avocado leaves are the traditional herb used to flavor Oaxacan black beans. If avocado leaves are not available, substitute 1 cup (250 mL) anise tea and reduce water by equal amount.

1 cup (250 mL) dried black beans

1 onion, chopped

2 garlic cloves, minced

1 tsp cumin seeds, toasted and ground

1–2 fresh epazote sprigs or 1 tsp dried epazote

2 Mexican avocado leaves or 1 cup (250 mL) anise tea (see note below)

sea salt, to taste

12 corn tortillas

8 oz (230 g) crumbled queso fresco or 1 cup (250 mL) Cashew Crema (p. 183)

1 Pickled Red Onion (p. 180), for garnish

Chiltepinera Hot Sauce (p. 173) or other salsa, for garnish

1 avocado, peeled, seeded, and sliced

4 cilantro sprigs

KABOCHA SQUASH IN PIPIAN VERDE

3–5 fresh poblano chiles

1 white onion, peeled and quartered

10 tomatillos, husks removed and rinsed

3 whole, unpeeled garlic cloves

1 4–5 lb (about 2 kg) kabocha squash

several tbsp of extra virgin coconut oil

sea salt and pepper, to taste

1 cup (250 mL) raw, hulled pumpkin seeds

2 cups (500 mL) vegetable stock or water

2 tbsp masa harina

½ tsp dried oregano, preferably Mexican

1 bunch cilantro (reserve a bit for garnish)

6–7 epazote sprigs, if available

½ bunch flat leaf parsley

2–4 leaves hoja santa or ¼ tsp anise seeds

1 tsp sea salt

¼ cup raw, hulled pumpkin seeds

¼ cup cilantro, leaves only

2 limes, quartered

Pipian verde is an herb-filled green sauce made with pumpkin seeds, often served with fish or poultry. In this vegan version, we serve a roasted kabocha squash in a bath of pipian verde. Serve with a side of beans and a pile of warm corn tortillas to sop up all of the yummy sauce.

....

Roast, peel, and seed poblano chiles according to one of the methods listed on p. 53. Preheat oven to broil.

On a rimmed cookie sheet, broil onions, tomatillos, and garlic until they just begin to char, about 10 minutes. Remove from oven and set aside. Set oven temperature to 400°F (200°C).

Kabocha skin is edible and tasty, so leave it on. Cut squash in half and remove seeds. Cut into 1-in (2.5-cm) wedges. Slather squash with coconut oil, salt, and pepper and place wedges on a cookie sheet lined with parchment paper. Bake for 30 minutes, turning after 15 minutes. Squash should pierce easily with a fork and show caramelization.

While squash is cooking, prepare sauce. In a dry, hot frying pan on medium heat, toast pumpkin seeds until they start to puff up or turn brown, about 3 minutes. In a blender, pulse pumpkin seeds with stock. Peel charred garlic and place in blender with 1 chile, onions, tomatillos, masa harina, oregano, cilantro, epazote, parsley, and hoja santa or anise. Purée until completely smooth. Add salt and remainder of chiles to taste and blend once more. This sauce should have a pleasant warmth. Although poblanos are usually quite mild, they can vary so it is best to add them slowly and taste after each addition until desired level of heat is obtained.

....

Pour sauce into a Dutch oven or large saucepan.
Simmer gently on medium heat for about 15 minutes,
stirring occasionally to prevent sticking. Serve by placing a generous portion of sauce in each bowl. Place
roasted squash on top and garnish with pumpkins
seeds, cilantro leaves, and a lime wedge to squeeze
over.

makes 6–8 servings

1 white onion, peeled and quartered

4 whole, unpeeled garlic cloves

6 dried ancho chiles, stems and seeds removed

3 whole cloves

5 whole allspice berries

¼ cup (60 mL) roasted peanuts

½ tsp ground cinnamon, preferably Ceylon or canela Mexicana

1 15-oz (425-g) can organic pumpkin purée or 2 cups (500 mL) roasted pumpkin (see p. 54–55), puréed

3 cups (750 mL) vegetable stock

1 small (about 1 oz [30g]) cone piloncillo

1 ½ tsp sea salt, or more to taste

about 2 tbsp extra virgin coconut oil, for griddle

12–18 corn tortillas

12 oz (340 g) queso Oaxaca, torn into strips or 2 cups (500 mL) finely diced roasted pumpkin, for filling

1 Pickled Red Onion (p. 180)

¼ cup cilantro leaves

ENMOLADAS: TORTILLAS SMOTHERED IN PUMPKIN MOLE

In even the smallest open-air markets in Mexico, vendors sell a dozen different mole pastes: yellow, red, green, brown, and black. From the Nahuatl word molli, meaning sauce or paste, mole is made of chiles, spices, seeds, and nuts. The chocolate-based mole of Puebla is best known outside of Mexico, but the varieties are truly endless. In this dish, tortillas are smothered in a pumpkin sauce spiced with peanuts, ancho chiles, and allspice.

....

To make mole:

On a dry griddle on medium heat, toast onions and garlic until charred on most sides. Allow garlic to cool and then snip ends and squeeze out roasted cloves. On same griddle, toast ancho chiles for about 1 minute per side, taking care not to burn. Put chiles in a bowl and cover with boiling water. Use a small plate to keep chiles submerged for 30 minutes. Drain chiles, reserving liquid. Remove and discard stems and seeds. Put chiles in a blender.

On same griddle, toast cloves and allspice berries for about 1 minute or until fragrant. Remove from heat. Add onions, garlic, chiles, ½ cup (125 mL) chile soaking liquid, cloves, allspice, peanuts, cinnamon, pumpkin, stock, piloncillo, and salt to a high-speed blender and purée until smooth. (If high-speed blender is not available, first dissolve piloncillo in 1 cup [250 mL] hot stock before adding to blender.) Be careful when blending hot liquids! In a large pot on medium heat, cook puréed mixture for about 20 minutes, stirring occasionally.

To assemble:

Preheat oven to 350°F (180°C).

Pour a generous ladle of mole into 9 x 13 in (3.5 L) baking dish.

Coat griddle with about 1 tsp oil at a time, as needed, and heat on medium. Heat 1 tortilla on griddle, flipping after about 1 minute. When heated through, use tongs to gently dip tortilla in mole sauce. Place in baking dish, top with several strips of cheese (or diced pumpkin, for vegan version), and roll into cigar shape. Repeat until pan is full. Ladle 1 cup (250 mL) mole on top of rolled enmoladas. Sprinkle with remainder of cheese, cover with foil, and bake for 20 minutes. Remove foil and bake for 5 more minutes. To serve, garnish with Pickled Red Onions and cilantro leaves.

For a vegan option, start with a 4–5 lb (about 2 kg) pumpkin—enough for both sauce and filling.

HUARACHES DE NOPAL

8 medium nopal paddles,
   cleaned and spines removed

1 tbsp extra virgin coconut oil

4 cups (1 L) cooked Black Velvet
   Beans (p. 154)

4 cups (1 L) shredded romaine
   lettuce or Red Cabbage Slaw
   (p. 135)

Chipotle Salsa (p. 168) or store-
   bought sauce, to taste

6 oz (175 g) crumbled *queso
   fresco* or ½ cup (125 mL)
   Cashew Crema (p. 183)

Huaraches are traditionally made with corn masa formed into a thick oval that resembles a huarache or sandal. In our version, we use a roasted nopal paddle as the "sandal sole" that provides the base for beans, cheese, and salsa. This is a great meal for anyone struggling with diabetes, as the nopales are low-carb and provide blood sugar-balancing properties.

....

Bring a large pot of water to a boil on high heat and add nopales. Cook for about 5 minutes. Remove and rinse under cool water. Pat dry. Lightly score and smear coconut oil on each side of nopal. On a dry griddle on high heat, cook nopales in batches (don't overcrowd in pan). Cook each side for about 3–5 minutes or until nopales begin to blister slightly. Set aside.

In a frying pan on medium heat, mash beans and cook until consistency of a loose paste, about 5 minutes.

Place nopales on a serving platter. Spread a layer of beans on each and serve topped with lettuce or slaw, salsa, and either cheese or Cashew Crema.

GRILL OPTION:

Use a gas grill or outdoor barbecue to cook whole raw nopal paddles: Rub paddles with oil to prevent sticking; scoring is not necessary. Grill nopal paddles about 7 minutes per side on medium high heat.

AMARANTH PANCAKES WITH MUSHROOMS & RAJAS

These savory pancakes are full of the fruits of the earth. This recipe uses whole grain amaranth for the base, enlivened by the umami flavor of mushrooms, the heartiness of the grated potato, and the smoky mild heat of the rajas (strips of roasted green chile). Serve with Pachamama Salad (p. 78) for an elegant dinner.

In a small saucepan on high heat, bring 2 cups (500 mL) water and lemon zest to a boil. Pour amaranth in a steady stream into boiling water and stir. Return to a boil, cover, and reduce heat to low. Cook for 20 minutes. Remove from heat and let stand for 10 minutes.

In a frying pan on medium heat, sauté mushrooms in oil. Season with salt and pepper and sauté for about 20 minutes, stirring occasionally and allowing mushrooms to brown.

Squeeze liquid from grated potatoes. In a mixing bowl, combine potatoes, onions, masa harina, egg, coriander, cumin, salt, pepper, thyme, and amaranth. Mixture should have consistency of cookie dough; if too loose, add a bit more masa harina. Allow mixture to rest for about 5 minutes.

Heat a large griddle on high heat for 3 minutes. Brush a small amount of oil on griddle. Drop 1 heaping tbsp amaranth mixture onto griddle. Reduce heat to medium. Using back of spoon, gently press mixture down to form a pancake. Repeat process, being sure not to crowd pan. Pancakes should be about 2 ½–3 in (6.35–8 cm) in diameter. Cook on each side for about 4 minutes, until they form a nice crust on each side.

zest of 1 lemon

1 cup (250 mL) amaranth

1 lb (500 g) in-season wild mushrooms

2 tbsp extra virgin coconut oil

¼ tsp salt

⅛ tsp white pepper

1 cup (250 mL) grated red potato

½ small onion, minced

¾ cup (60 mL) masa harina

1 egg, beaten

1 tsp coriander seeds, toasted and ground

1 tsp cumin seeds, toasted and ground

1 tsp salt

⅛ tsp white pepper

½ tsp dried thyme

1 tbsp extra virgin coconut oil, for griddle

3 fresh New Mexico or Anaheim green chiles, roasted, peeled, and torn into small strips

5 oz (150 g) goat cheese (optional)

CONTINUED ▶

▶▶ To serve, place pancake on each plate with a generous heap of mushrooms and several strips of chiles on top. Place another pancake on top and add more mushrooms and chile strips. Repeat once more so you have a stack of three pancakes. Top stacks with goat cheese.

CHAPTER SEVEN

Tacos, Tlacoyos & Tamales

HIBISCUS FLOWER TACOS

makes 8 tacos

Believe it or not, the hibiscus flowers give a meaty texture to these tacos. The flowers are tart, which plays nicely with the potatoes, chipotle, and honey. Dried hibiscus flowers are widely available in Mexican markets and are an excellent food for heart health!

....

In a small saucepan on medium-high heat, place flowers, honey, and 2 cups (500 mL) water and simmer for 25 minutes. Meanwhile, in a frying pan on medium, melt coconut oil. Sauté onions in coconut oil until translucent, about 5 minutes. Strain flowers, reserving liquid for another use (see below.) Chop flowers coarsely and add to onions. Stir in potatoes and garlic and sauté mixture for about 5 minutes, stirring often. Add minced chipotle, salt, pepper and ½ cup (125 mL) water. Cover and cook for 15 minutes, or until potatoes are cooked through. Remove from heat, stir in lime juice, and adjust seasonings.

Heat a griddle on high for 5 minutes. Reduce heat to medium, and heat tortillas 1–2 minutes on each side. Divide potato mixture between 8 tortillas. Garnish each taco with a spoonful of salsa, several cubes of avocado, a sprig of cilantro, and a smattering of *queso fresco.*

After soaking flowers in water, save bright red water. Taste and add more sugar, honey, or stevia to taste. It should still be tangy. Drink hot or cold. This beverage, also called jamaica, has been used medicinally to treat high cholesterol and hypertension.

½ cup (125 mL) dried hibiscus flowers

2 tsp raw local honey

1 tbsp extra virgin coconut oil

½ white onion, diced

2 large red potatoes, scrubbed and diced

2 garlic cloves, minced

1 tbsp minced Chipotles en Adobo (p. 167 or use canned)

¾ tsp sea salt

⅛ tsp white pepper

½ tsp lime juice

8 corn tortillas

Chipotle Salsa (p. 168) or store-bought

1 large avocado, peeled, seeded, and cubed

8 cilantro sprigs

4 oz (115g) crumbled *queso fresco* (optional)

makes 6–8 servings

TACOS DE QUELITES

1 tbsp extra virgin coconut oil

1 fresh jalapeño, veined, seeded, and diced (reserve some seeds)

5 garlic cloves, peeled and minced

5 cups (1.25 L) quelites (lamb's quarters) or spinach, washed and drained

6–8 corn tortillas

1 avocado, peeled, seeded, and cubed

1 cup Pico de Gallo (p. 169)

3 oz (90 g) crumbled queso fresco

Our grandmothers were always on the lookout for quelites *(lamb's quarters), which they cooked up with chile seeds and a bit of fat. Rich in minerals,* quelites *are fortifying, and have been studied for their many disease-fighting properties. When* quelites *were unavailable, our grandmothers substituted spinach.*

....

In a large frying pan on medium, heat oil. Sauté jalapeño and a few seeds for about 4 minutes. Add garlic and stir until fragrant, about 1 minute. Add *quelites* and stir to combine. Cook *quelites* until soft, about 10 minutes (less time for spinach). If necessary, add a few tbsp water to prevent greens from sticking to pan.

Heat a griddle on high for 3–5 minutes. Reduce heat to medium and heat tortillas, about 1–2 minutes per side. To assemble tacos, place a heaping spoonful of greens in center of each tortilla, top with cubes of avocado, a spoonful of Pico de Gallo and a smattering of cheese.

SWEET POTATO TACOS WITH RED CABBAGE SLAW

These tacos are a nicely balanced bite: you get sweet, crunchy, creamy, and spicy all at the same time!

....

Preheat oven to 400°F (200°C).

In a mixing bowl, thoroughly toss sweet potatoes with oil, salt, pepper, and chipotle. Place in a 9 x 13 in (3.5 L) baking dish and bake for 30–45 minutes, or until sweet potatoes are cooked through.

Heat dry griddle on high for 3–5 minutes. Reduce heat to medium and warm tortillas, about 1–2 minutes per side. Assemble tacos by placing a spoonful of sweet potatoes on each tortilla. Top each taco with cabbage slaw, Cashew Crema, and salsa.

Red Cabbage Slaw

In a salad bowl, toss together cabbage, carrots, cilantro, and green onions. In a small bowl, whisk together remainder of ingredients to make a light dressing. Toss cabbage mixture with dressing. Taste and adjust seasonings.

2 sweet potatoes, peeled and diced

2 tbsp olive oil

1 tsp sea salt

¼ tsp white pepper

¼ tsp ground chipotle

10 corn tortillas

Red Cabbage Slaw (recipe below)

1 cup (250 mL) Cashew Crema (p. 183)

1 cup (250 mL) Chipotle Salsa (p. 168) or store-bought

Red Cabbage Slaw:

½ head red cabbage, cored and finely shredded

1 large carrot, cut into fine julienne

¼ cup (60 mL) chopped cilantro leaves

1 bunch green onions, diced

1 tbsp lime juice

1 tbsp orange juice

½ tsp pure maple syrup

1 tbsp extra virgin olive oil

1 garlic clove, peeled and minced

½ tsp sea salt

¼ tsp white pepper

makes 8 tacos

TURNIP GREEN TACOS

1 tsp salt

1 dried chipotle chile

1 small (about 1 oz [30 g]) cone
   piloncillo

8 cups (2 L) turnip greens,
   washed

1 tbsp extra virgin coconut oil

5 garlic cloves, peeled and
   minced

½ tsp salt

⅛ tsp pepper

8 corn tortillas

2 avocados, peeled, seeded, and
   sliced

Pickled Red Onions (p. 180)

½ cup (125 mL) Roasted
   Guajillo Salsa (p. 170) or
   store-bought

4 oz (115 g) crumbled queso
   cotija (optional)

One day our neighbor Jenn gifted us a huge bag of turnip greens from her garden. Luz developed this recipe, treating the greens almost like collards, so that when you eat them, they melt in your mouth! This recipe has become such a favorite that we now grow our own turnip greens just for tacos. Turnip greens are a cruciferous vegetable with tremendous anti-cancer benefits.

....

In a large pot on high heat, bring 6 cups (1 ½ L) water with 1 tsp salt to a boil. Add chipotle and *piloncillo* and stir to combine. Add turnip greens and cook for 20 minutes or until greens are very soft. Strain greens and allow to cool slightly. Coarsely chop.

In a frying pan on medium heat, melt oil. When oil is warm, add garlic and cook for 1 minute to release aroma. Add greens and sauté for about 10 minutes. Season with salt and pepper and remove from heat.

Heat a griddle on high for 3–5 minutes. Reduce heat to medium and warm tortillas, about 1–2 minutes per side. To assemble tacos, place an equal portion of greens on each tortilla. Top with slices of avocado, a few slices of pickled onions, about 1 tsp salsa, and a few crumbles of cheese.

TACOS DE MI CORAZÓN

The texture and taste of the hearts of palm in these tacos is reminiscent of pulled pork. In general, we're not fans of "fake meat" products, which tend to be highly processed. We slow roast the hearts of palm, with plenty of spices, to make a plant-based taco with a spicy, hearty, meaty flavor.

....

Preheat oven to 275°F (140°C).

Cut each heart of palm in half. Tear each half into 4–5 strips and set aside.

In a frying pan on medium, heat oil. Sauté onions, chiles de árbol, cinnamon, and bay leaf for 5 minutes, stirring often. Add garlic and sauté for 1 minute. Add cumin, coriander, jumpier berries, allspice, salt, pepper, and oregano, and stir well with wooden spoon to coat onion with spices. Add hearts of palm, tomato sauce, 1 cup (250 mL) water, lime zest, and orange and lime juice. Stir gently to combine. Transfer mixture to a greased 1 ½ quart (1.4 L) casserole dish. Cover and bake for 90 minutes, stirring every 30 minutes. Remove from oven and remove cinnamon stick, bay leaf, and chiles de árbol.

Heat a griddle on high for 3–5 minutes. Reduce heat to medium and warm tortillas, about 1–2 minutes per side. To assemble tacos, place a spoonful of hearts of palm mixture on each tortilla. Garnish each taco with cilantro and minced onions.

1 14-oz (400-g) can hearts of palm, drained

1 tbsp olive oil

¼ white onion, minced

2 whole dried chiles de árbol

½ cinnamon stick, preferably Ceylon or canela Mexicana

1 bay leaf

2 garlic cloves, peeled and minced

1 tsp cumin seeds, toasted and ground

1 tsp coriander seeds, toasted and ground

8 juniper berries, toasted and ground

3 allspice berries, toasted and ground

1 tsp sea salt

¼ tsp white pepper

1 tsp dried oregano, preferably Mexican

1 8-oz (227-g) can tomato sauce

¼ tsp lime zest

1 tbsp orange juice

1 tsp lime juice

8 corn tortillas

½ bunch cilantro, chopped, for garnish

½ onion, minced, for garnish

TLACOYOS CON NOPALES

2 tbsp extra virgin coconut oil

2 garlic cloves, peeled and chopped

¼ white onion, diced

2 cups (500 mL) cleaned, de-spined, and diced nopal paddles

1 fresh jalapeño, diced

1 tsp sea salt

2 tbsp non-hydrogenated shortening

¾ tsp salt

2 cups (500 mL) fresh masa for tortillas or 1 ¾ cups (415 mL) masa harina and 1 cup + 2 tbsp (266 mL) warm water

6 heaping tbsp Requesón de Semillas de Calabaza (p. 184) or 6 tbsp goat cheese

1 ½ cups (375 mL) Roasted Guajillo Salsa (p. 170) or store-bought

1 avocado, peeled, seeded, and thinly sliced

1 cup (250 mL) Fermented Red Cabbage Curtido (p. 181) or Red Cabbage Slaw (p. 135)

Tlacoyos are oval-shaped stuffed corn cakes with slightly pointed ends. In Mexico City, they are cooked and sold on street corners and in open-air markets, as they have been for hundreds of years. In this version, we stuff the tlacoyos with pumpkin seed "cheese" and serve them topped with guacamole, nopales, and red cabbage. Note: A tortilla press is used to make these tlacoyos.

....

In a frying pan with a tight-fitting lid on high, heat oil until it just begins to shimmer. Reduce heat to low, add garlic, and swirl to release aroma, about 15 seconds. Stir in onions, nopales, chile, and salt. Cover and cook for 10 minutes or until nopales are tender and still very juicy. Remove lid and continue to cook until all liquid evaporates, 20–30 minutes. If nopales are still juicy, increase heat to high and stir until all liquid evaporates.

To prepare masa for tlacoyos: In a large bowl, combine shortening and salt. Using fingers, fluff up the shortening. Add fresh masa or masa harina. If using masa harina, slowly pour in warm water while working masa with hands. The dough will begin to come together. Continue to knead masa and add warm water by the spoonful, if needed, until masa is soft but not sticky.

Divide dough into 6 equal portions. Shape each portion into a ball and roll between hands to create a log shape about 3 ½ in (9 cm) long. Cut a thin plastic produce bag into 2 sheets. Place 1 sheet on bottom half of tortilla press. Place masa log in center of press, parallel to lever and cover with second sheet of plastic. Gently close, pressing lever to flatten masa to an oblong shape

about 5–6 in (12–15 cm) long. Open press and carefully peel off top sheet of plastic. Visualize a horizontal line dividing masa in half lengthwise. This will be the fold line. Place 1 tbsp *requesón* below line but away from edges. Using bottom layer of plastic to help, fold masa over filling until edges meet. Using fingers over plastic sheet, press edges to seal. Press tlacoyo gently so that it forms a flat, oblong pancake.

Heat a large, dry griddle on medium-high for at least 3 minutes. Reduce heat to medium-low and gently set tlacoyo on griddle. In 30–60 seconds, tlacoyo should easily release from griddle. Turn over and cook on second side for 4–6 minutes. Flip and cook first side for same amount of time. Continue to cook and flip until tlacoyos are a pale golden-brown color on both sides. Remove from heat. Spread a generous spoonful of salsa on top of each tlacoyo. Top with 2 tbsp nopales, a few avocado slices, and curtido.

TLACOYOS CON QUELITES

These tlacoyos were inspired by a recipe from Mexican chef Yuri de Gortari Krauss. Stuffed with beans and topped with sautéed greens, they make a highly nutritious and satisfying supper. This dish is a tasty way to use up leftover beans. Note: A tortilla press is used to make these tlacoyos.

....

In a frying pan with a tight-fighting lid on medium, heat oil. Sauté onions until translucent, about 5 minutes. Add garlic and cook for 1 minute. Stir in greens, salt, and pepper and cover pan. Cook for 10 minutes or until greens are tender. Remove from heat and set aside.

In a frying pan on medium, gently warm oil and add beans. Mash well and cook until beans are warm and have the consistency of a paste. Remove from heat and set aside.

To prepare masa for tlacoyos: In a large bowl, combine shortening and salt. Using fingers, fluff up the shortening. Add fresh masa or masa harina. If using masa harina, slowly pour in warm water while working masa with hands. The dough will begin to come together. Continue to knead masa and add warm water by the spoonful, if needed, until masa is soft but not sticky.

Divide dough into 6 equal portions. Shape each portion into a ball and roll between hands to create a log shape about 3 ½ in (9 cm) long. Cut a thin plastic produce bag into 2 sheets. Place 1 sheet on bottom half of tortilla press. Place masa log in center of press, parallel to lever and cover with second sheet of plastic. Gently close, pressing lever to flatten masa to an oblong shape about 5–6 in (12–15 cm) long. Open press and carefully peel off top sheet of

Ingredients

- 1 tbsp olive oil
- ¼ white onion, diced
- 2 garlic cloves, peeled and chopped
- 4 cups (1 L) quelites (lamb's quarters) or 1 large bunch Swiss chard, stems removed
- ½ tsp sea salt
- ¼ tsp white pepper
- 1 tbsp olive oil
- 1 cup (250 mL) Old School Pinto Beans (p: 151)
- 2 cups (500 mL) fresh masa for tortillas or 1 ¾ cups (415 mL) masa harina and 1 cup + 2 tbsp (266 mL) warm water
- 2 tbsp non-hydrogenated shortening
- ¾ tsp sea salt
- Roasted Guajillo Salsa (p. 170) or store-bought salsa
- 4 oz (115 g) crumbled queso cotija (optional)

CONTINUED ▶

▶▶ plastic. Visualize a horizontal line dividing masa in half lengthwise. This will be the fold line. Place 1 tbsp beans below line but away from edges. Using bottom layer of plastic to help, fold masa over filling until edges meet. Using fingers over plastic sheet, press edges to seal. Press tlacoyo gently so that it forms a flat, oblong pancake.

Heat a large, dry griddle on medium-high for at least 3 minutes. Reduce heat to medium-low and gently set tlacoyo on griddle. In 30–60 seconds, tlacoyo should easily release from griddle. Turn over and cook on second side for 4–6 minutes. Flip and cook first side for same amount of time. Continue to cook and flip until tlacoyos are a pale golden-brown color on both sides. Remove from heat and spread a generous spoonful of salsa on each tlacoyo, place sautéed greens on top, and sprinkle greens with cheese.

BUTTERNUT SQUASH & ROASTED GREEN CHILE TAMALITOS

Tamales (tamalli *in Nahuatl) are a favorite food for holidays: we like to enlist friends and family to help assemble them, and the work goes quickly as the conversation flows. Luz's grandmother often made green chile and cheese tamales: in our vegan version, we use butternut squash instead of cheese. We make our tamales on the small side, hence the name* tamalitos *(little tamales).*

....

I. Prepare Filling

Cut squash into quarters and scoop out seeds. Using a potato peeler, remove skin. Cut each quarter in half. In a large saucepan on medium heat, combine squash, garlic, onions, cumin, allspice, thyme, and salt. Cover with water and cook for 20–25 minutes or until squash is fork-tender. Strain squash and reserve 1 cup (125 mL) stock. Reserve 1 piece of squash to blend. Dice remainder of squash, place in bowl, and set aside.

In a blender, purée piece of squash, reserved stock, onions, and garlic until smooth. Set aside.

Tear chiles into thin strips, about ¼–½ in (6 mm–1 cm) wide (about 12 strips per chile), place in a bowl, and set aside.

2. Prepare Masa

Using a hand or stand mixer, whip shortening for 5 minutes, or until doubled in size. Add salt and baking powder and whip into shortening. Add masa and blended stock mixture, a bit at a time. When mixture becomes too thick to beat with hand mixer (if using), hand

Filling:

1 butternut squash, about 1 lb (500 g)

3 garlic cloves, peeled

1 white onion, quartered

1 tsp cumin seeds, toasted and ground

8 allspice berries, toasted and ground

½ tsp dried thyme

1 tsp sea salt

6 fresh poblano chiles, roasted and peeled

Masa:

1 cup (250 mL) non-hydrogenated shortening

1 tbsp sea salt

1 tbsp aluminum-free baking powder

3 lb (1 ½ kg) masa for tamales (without added salt or shortening)

3 dozen corn husks, rinsed, soaked in hot water, and patted dry

CONTINUED ▶

▶▶ knead for about 20 minutes. At first, masa may be sticky; as it is worked, the liquid will be absorbed and it will become less sticky. Place a pea-size piece into a glass of cool water to see if it floats. If it doesn't float, continue to knead or add more shortening or more liquid, as needed.

3. Assemble Tamalitos

Set out ingredients (squash, chile strips, masa), each in a separate bowl. Take a corn husk: notice that it is vaguely triangular and that one side is smoother than the other (which has more pronounced ridges). Lay husk out before you, smooth side up, and base of triangle at top. Place a scant ¼ cup (60 mL) masa on corn husk. With a spoon or fingers, spread masa to create a rectangle about 3 x 5 in (8 x 12 cm) and about ⅛-in (3-mm) thick. Leave a ½-in (1-cm) border at top, ¼ in (6 mm) on each side, and about 1 in (2.5 cm) at bottom. Leave narrow point of triangle entirely free of masa. Place 2–3 strips chile and 5–6 pieces squash in center of rectangle. Bring 2 sides together, folding 1 side over the other. Fold bottom point up. Tamales are now open at top and enclosed on the other 3 sides. Place in a baking dish, open end on top. Repeat until you have used up either masa, corn husks, or filling.

4. Cook Tamalitos

In a tamale pot or large pot with a steamer, add 3–4 in (about 9–10 cm) water. Stack tamales in steamer, open end up. Place a wet dish towel over tamales to keep steam in, and cover with pot lid. Bring to a boil, lower heat to medium-low, and steam for 45–60 minutes. Remove tamales from heat and check one. If it releases easily from side of corn husk, tamales are done. If they appear a bit mushy, cover and let sit for 30 minutes. Overcooked tamales become rubbery, so don't overcook.

RED CHILE XOCOTETL TAMALITOS

Another favorite tamale variety we grew up eating was red chile and roasted pork or beef. This recipe is a vegan take on our abuelitas' meat tamales: young jackfruit cooked in red chile adds a shredded meat texture. We pair the green fruit (xocotetl in Nahuatl) with a tasty mixture of potatoes, capers, and olives.

....

1. Prepare Filling

Parboil potatoes for 5 minutes, strain, and set aside. In a medium frying pan on medium heat, sauté onions and garlic in coconut oil. Rinse jackfruit in cold water and tear into ¼ in (6 mm) strips. Add jackfruit to onion and garlic mixture. Season with salt, pepper, and cumin and cook for 5 minutes. Add 1 ½ cups (375 mL) Classic Red Chile Sauce and simmer mixture for 10 minutes. Remove from heat and set aside. Place olives and capers in 2 small bowls. Reserve ½ cup (125 mL) sauce, and put remainder in a bowl.

2. Prepare Masa

Using a hand or stand mixer, whip shortening for 5 minutes, or until doubled in size. Add salt and baking powder and whip into shortening. Add masa and ½ cup (125 mL) Classic Red Chile Sauce, a bit at a time. When mixture becomes too thick to beat with hand mixer (if using), hand knead for about 20 minutes. At first, masa may be sticky; as it is worked, the liquid will be absorbed and it will become less sticky. Place a pea-size piece into a glass of cool water to see if it floats. If it doesn't float, continue to knead or add more shortening or more liquid, as needed.

Filling:

5 red potatoes, scrubbed and diced

1 onion, diced

3 garlic cloves, peeled and minced

1 tbsp coconut oil

2 20-oz (565-g) cans young green jackfruit in brine, drained!

½ tsp sea salt

⅛ tsp white pepper

½ tsp cumin seeds, toasted and ground

4 cups (1 L) Classic Red Chile Sauce (p. 175)

18 pitted green olives, halved and drained

½ cup (125 mL) capers, rinsed

Masa:

1 cup (250 mL) non-hydrogenated vegetable shortening

1 tbsp sea salt

1 tbsp aluminum-free baking powder

3 lb (1 ½ kg) fresh masa for tamales (without added salt or shortening)

3 dozen corn husks, rinsed, soaked in hot water, and patted dry

CONTINUED ▶

▶▶ 3. Assemble Tamalitos

Set out ingredients (jackfruit mixture, potatoes, olives, capers, sauce, and masa), each in a separate bowl. Take a corn husk: notice that it is vaguely triangular and that one side is smoother than the other (which has more pronounced ridges). Lay husk out before you, smooth side up, and base of triangle at top. Place a scant ¼ cup (60 mL) masa on corn husk. With a spoon or fingers, spread masa to create a rectangle about 3 x 5 in (8 x 12 cm) and about ⅛ in (3 mm) thick. Leave a ½ in (1 cm) border at top, ¼ in (6 mm) on each side, and about 1 in (2.5 cm) at bottom. Leave narrow point of triangle entirely free of masa. Place 1 tbsp jackfruit mixture, 4 pieces potato, ½ olive, 4 capers, and 1 tbsp sauce in center of rectangle. Bring 2 sides together, folding 1 side over the other. Fold bottom point up. Tamales are now open at top and enclosed on the other 3 sides. Place in a baking dish, open end on top. Repeat until you have used up either masa, corn husks, or filling.

4. Cook Tamalitos

In a tamale pot or large pot with a steamer, add 3–4 in (about 9–10 cm) water. Stack tamales in steamer, open end up. Place a wet dish towel over tamales to keep steam in, and cover with pot lid. Bring to a boil, lower heat to medium-low, and steam for 45–60 minutes. Remove tamales from heat and check one. If it releases easily from side of corn husk, tamales are done. If they appear a bit mushy, cover and let sit for 30 minutes. Overcooked tamales become rubbery, so don't overcook.

CHAPTER EIGHT

A la Carta: Beans, Tortillas &
Vegetable Sides

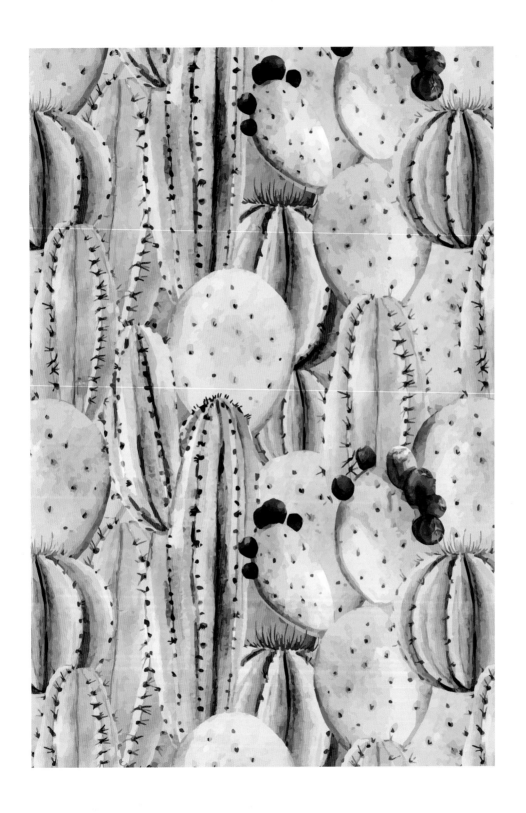

OLD SCHOOL PINTO BEANS

makes 6 cups (1 ½ L) or about 8 servings

Nothing is more comforting than the smell of a freshly cooked pot of beans. Try to find the freshest dried beans you can: they'll be creamy and delicious when you cook them. Eating beans several times a week reduces your risk of heart disease and diabetes and has been shown to lower cholesterol.

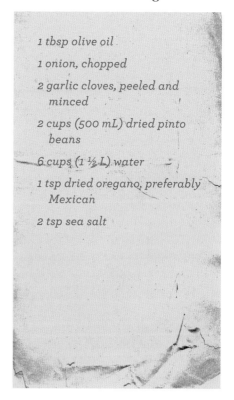

1 tbsp olive oil

1 onion, chopped

2 garlic cloves, peeled and minced

2 cups (500 mL) dried pinto beans

6 cups (1 ½ L) water

1 tsp dried oregano, preferably Mexican

2 tsp sea salt

In a frying pan on medium, heat oil. Sauté onions and garlic for about 5 minutes. Transfer onion mixture, along with beans, water, and oregano to a slow cooker. Cook beans on high heat for 4–6 hours or on low for 6–9 hours, or until skins are soft and insides are creamy. When beans are almost done, add salt and allow to continue to cook for at least 20 minutes to allow beans to absorb salt.

Serve beans whole, in their stock. When beans are served straight from the pot, they are called *de olla*. We often eat our beans this way, either serving up a big bowl for dinner or in small bowls to accompany a meal. Alternately, you can gently mash the beans in the pot until they are creamy and still soupy. (This was Luz's grandmother's preferred method.) To achieve a paste-like consistency, many cooks fry their beans in oil. Instead, we transfer beans to a dry frying pan on medium heat to mash them and allow them to reduce.

Embrace bean diversity! Use another spotted bean, such as Ojo de Cabra, Snow Cap, Jacob's Cattle, Calypso, Cranberry, Good Mother Stallard, or Anasazi beans in place of pintos. Although these beans look different from one another in their dried state, once cooked they all look a lot like pintos.

SOLDADERA BEANS

makes 6 cups (1 ½ L) or about 8 servings

This recipe is our feminist riff on the common frijoles charros (cowboy beans). A vegan dish named after the women who fought in the Mexican Revolution (soldaderas), this features a smoky flavor—as if cooked over a camp fire.

....

In a large frying pan on medium heat, melt coconut oil. Add onions and cook for about 5 minutes. Add bell peppers and cook for 5 minutes. Add garlic, cumin, and coriander and cook until fragrance is released, about 1 minute. Pour in beer and stir in oregano, bay leaves, liquid smoke, and chipotle. Bring up to a slow simmer.

Transfer mixture, along with beans and water, to slow cooker. Cook beans on high heat for 4–6 hours or low 6–9 hours, or until skins are soft and insides are creamy. Add tomatoes, cilantro, and salt. Reduce heat to low (if necessary) and cook 1 hour to allow tomatoes to soften and seasonings to meld.

SHOPPING NOTE:

We use a pure-brewed organic lager in this recipe. A Mexican beer would also work well.

1 tbsp extra virgin coconut oil

2 white onions, peeled and chopped

1 orange or yellow bell pepper, diced

1 head garlic (about 14 cloves), peeled and chopped

1 tsp cumin seeds, toasted and ground

1 tsp coriander seeds, toasted and ground

1 12-oz (355-mL) bottle lager beer (see Shopping Note)

1 tbsp dried oregano, preferably Mexican

2 bay leaves

¼ tsp liquid smoke concentrate (optional)

1 tbsp minced Chipotles en Adobo (p. 167) or canned

2 cups (500 mL) heirloom beans (pinquito, bolita, vaquero, Good Mother Stallard, or pinto)

1 qt (1 L) water

4 Roma or plum tomatoes, chopped or 1 14.5-oz (411-g) can fire-roasted chopped tomatoes

½ cup (125 mL) chopped cilantro

2 tsp sea salt

BLACK VELVET BEANS

2 cups (500 mL) dried black
   beans, sorted and rinsed

6 cups (1 ½ L) water

2 Mexican avocado leaves

1 tbsp dried epazote

1 white onion, diced

1 yellow bell pepper, stems and
   seeds removed, and diced

1 tbsp extra virgin coconut oil

4 garlic cloves, peeled and
   minced

1 tbsp minced Chipotles en
   Adobo (p. 167) or canned

1 tbsp cumin seeds, toasted and
   ground

2 tsp sea salt

3 tbsp sour orange juice (or
   2 tbsp orange juice + 1 tbsp
   lime juice)

¼ cup (60 mL) fresh cilantro
   leaves

*Catriona first tasted delicious black beans on a childhood trip to the
Yucatán. Luz's recipe brings together the flavors of Mexico's Gulf Coast
with the anise-like flavor of Mexican avocado leaves and the tang of sour
oranges. These beans have a delightful velvety texture.*

In a slow cooker on high heat, add beans and water.

On a griddle on high heat, toast avocado leaves for a few seconds on
each side, until aroma is released. Using fingers, crumble into bean
pot, along with epazote.

In a large frying pan on medium heat, sauté onions and bell peppers
in oil until soft, about 10 minutes. Add garlic, chipotle, and cumin and
sauté for 1 minute. Transfer mixture to bean pot. Cook beans on high
for 4–6 hours or low 6–9 hours, or until skins are soft and insides
are creamy. Add salt and cook, uncovered, for 20 minutes. Before
serving, stir in sour orange juice and garnish with cilantro leaves.

CORN TORTILLAS

makes about 10
6-in (15-cm) tortillas

Corn tortillas are the heart of a decolonized diet. We encourage you to take the time to make your own tortillas, at least once in a while. Whether you use fresh masa or dried masa harina they will be so much more flavorful than store-bought! Eat them as is to serve with stews or beans, or use them in any of our taco recipes. Note: A tortilla press is used to make these.

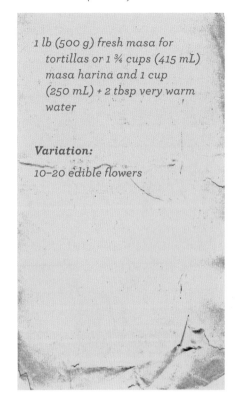

1 lb (500 g) fresh masa for tortillas or 1 ¾ cups (415 mL) masa harina and 1 cup (250 mL) + 2 tbsp very warm water

Variation:

10–20 edible flowers

CONTINUED ▶

....

If using fresh masa, dough needs to be kneaded for a few minutes to refresh. If using masa harina, place in large mixing bowl. Slowly pour in warm water while working flour with hands to create a dough. Knead until smooth, about 5 minutes. Dough should be soft but not sticky, like Play-Doh. If needed, add more water or masa harina to achieve the right consistency.

Heat griddle on high for at least 3 minutes. Press walnut-sized piece of dough into a flat disc. Cut a thin plastic produce bag into 2 sheets. Place 1 sheet on bottom half of tortilla press, and place disc in center of press. Place second sheet of plastic over disc. Using lever, gently close tortilla press to flatten masa. Leaving tortilla between plastic sheets, flip over and gently press again. With plastic in place, lift tortilla off press, and carefully peel off top sheet. Hold tortilla in left hand (if you are right-handed) with remaining plastic sheet facing up, and carefully peel off.

VARIATION:
After pressing tortilla in tortilla press, gently lift off top plastic sheet and press flowers into tortilla. Replace plastic and use tortilla press to very gently press flowers into tortilla. Proceed to make tortillas, as directed on following page.

▶▶ Hold raw tortilla in palm of hand and carefully slide (don't flip!) onto griddle. Reduce heat to medium. As soon as edges of tortilla start to turn up slightly and it releases from griddle (about 15–25 seconds), flip over. Continue to cook for 2–3 minutes. Flip tortilla again and cook until fully cooked on both sides, with no raw spots. Tortilla might puff up, which is a good thing. (To encourage puffing, press gently on edges of cooked side with a clean cloth.) If it doesn't puff up, don't worry.

Remove tortilla from griddle before it starts to crisp and while still pliable. Don't worry if tortilla isn't fully cooked in center. Place cooked tortilla inside a basket lined with a clean dishtowel, and flip edges of towel over to keep tortilla warm. Continue to make tortillas, add them to basket, and cover. Tortillas will continue to cook as they steam together in basket. By the time you serve them, they'll be perfect.

*makes about 12
6-in (15-cm) tortillas*

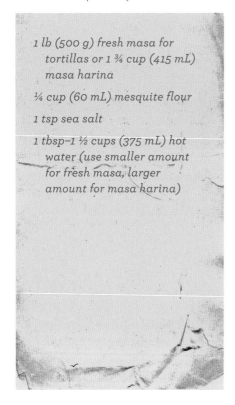

*1 lb (500 g) fresh masa for
tortillas or 1 ¾ cup (415 mL)
masa harina*

¼ cup (60 mL) mesquite flour

1 tsp sea salt

*1 tbsp–1 ½ cups (375 mL) hot
water (use smaller amount
for fresh masa, larger
amount for masa harina)*

MESQUITE CORN TORTILLAS

The mesquite in our recipes refers not to the wood smoke used to flavor barbeques but to the pods from mesquite trees that are ground into a flour. Mesquite has been eaten by Native peoples for centuries. The flour adds very subtle sweet and nutty notes, makes corn tortillas softer and more pliable, and also helps the body to balance blood sugar. Note: A tortilla press is used to make these.

....

If using fresh masa, place in a mixing bowl and knead a few times. Form into a ball, then indent with thumb. Place mesquite flour, salt, and 1 tbsp water in indentation, then knead well to incorporate mesquite. Add more water if needed to create a pliable dough. Follow directions for making corn tortillas on pp. 155–56.

If using masa harina, in a large bowl, combine masa harina, mesquite flour, and salt. Gradually add water to form a dough. Dough should hold together without sticking to hands. If dough is sticky, add more masa harina. Form walnut-sized balls and follow directions for making corn tortillas on pp. 155–56.

AMARANTH CORN TORTILLAS

This tortilla recipe was inspired by the characters Sister Salt and Indigo in Leslie Marmon Silko's novel Garden in the Dunes. The two girls were taught by their grandma how to seek out, harvest, and prepare the wild native foods. Silko writes: "As the amaranth went to seed, they took turns kneeling at the grinding stone, then Sister Salt made tortillas." Amaranth is a complete protein, high in calcium, and has been shown to reduce high blood pressure and high cholesterol, lower blood-glucose levels, exert anti-tumor activity, and protect the liver from alcohol damage. Note: A tortilla press is used to make these.

1 lb (500 g) fresh masa for tortillas or 1 ¾ cup (415 mL) masa harina

¼ cup (60 mL) amaranth flour

1 tsp sea salt

1 tbsp–1 ½ cups (375 mL) hot water (use smaller amount for fresh masa; larger amount for masa harina)

If using fresh masa, place in a mixing bowl and knead a few times. Form into a ball, then indent with thumb. Place amaranth flour, salt, and 1 tbsp water in indentation, then knead well to incorporate amaranth. Add more water if needed to create a pliable dough. Follow directions for making corn tortillas on pp. 155–56.

If using masa harina, in a large bowl, combine masa harina, amaranth flour, and salt. Gradually add water to form a dough. Dough should hold together without sticking to hands. If dough is sticky, add more masa harina. Form walnut-sized balls and follow directions for making corn tortillas on pp. 155–56.

makes 12–16 tortillas

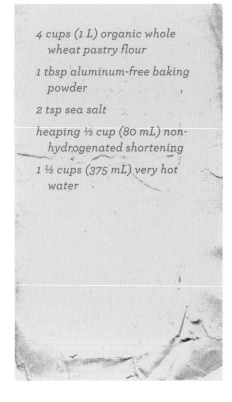

4 cups (1 L) organic whole
   wheat pastry flour

1 tbsp aluminum-free baking
   powder

2 tsp sea salt

heaping ⅓ cup (80 mL) non-
   hydrogenated shortening

1 ½ cups (375 mL) very hot
   water

BORDERLANDS WHOLE WHEAT TORTILLAS

This recipe is our homage to queer Chicana theorist and poet Gloria Anzaldúa, who says that to live in the borderlands means to eat whole wheat tortillas. Our recipe for flour tortillas came to us from our brother-in-law's mother, "Minnie" Reyes Wright. Because we advocate eating only whole grains, we adapted it to use whole wheat flour. Don't divide this recipe in half: you'll break the magic, and it just won't come out right.

In a large bowl, mix flour with baking powder and salt. When measuring shortening, make sure it's rounded well above the measuring cup. With a pastry cutter, cut shortening into flour mixture until you can no longer see shortening. Add hot water all at once, and mix well, then knead for 1–2 minutes. Dough should be soft and slightly sticky.

Place dough in a gallon ziplock bag and seal. Let sit for at least 30 minutes. Squeeze off 12–16 egg-size balls. Flour clean, flat surface. Sprinkle more flour over one ball of dough and press flat. Using a rolling pin, roll disc into a flat pancake about 8 in (20 cm) in diameter. Roll 1 side only: do not flip.

Heat a dry griddle for about 5 minutes on medium-high. Carefully transfer tortilla to griddle. Cook 1–2 minutes. Flip over and cook 1–2 minutes more. Remove tortilla, wrap in a clean dishcloth, and allow tortillas to steam together.

SKILLET CORNBREAD

We love cornbread with our chili beans, and if there's any left over, Catriona drizzles it with honey for dessert, and the next morning, Luz fries it up with butter for breakfast. Baking in a cast-iron frying pan provides an even heat and a golden crust. This recipe is naturally gluten free. The quinoa flour gives a light crumb while preserving the corn texture.

....

Preheat oven to 425°F (220°C).

In a large bowl, whisk together cornmeal, quinoa flour, salt, baking powder, and baking soda. In a separate bowl, beat eggs, then whisk in buttermilk. Add wet ingredients to dry ingredients and whisk until just blended. Add butter to a 9-in (23-cm) cast-iron frying pan and place in oven until butter melts. Remove from oven and pour all but about 1 tbsp butter into batter, gently folding it in. Pour batter into pan, reduce oven temperature to 375°F (190°C), and return pan to oven. Bake for 20–25 minutes, until edges start to brown and a toothpick inserted into center comes out clean. Cool for 10 minutes and serve straight from pan.

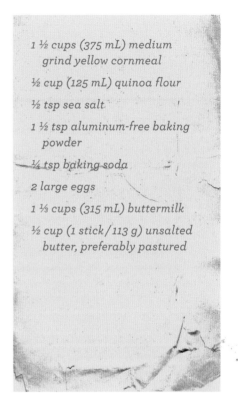

1 ½ cups (375 mL) medium grind yellow cornmeal

½ cup (125 mL) quinoa flour

½ tsp sea salt

1 ½ tsp aluminum-free baking powder

¼ tsp baking soda

2 large eggs

1 ⅓ cups (315 mL) buttermilk

½ cup (1 stick / 113 g) unsalted butter, preferably pastured

makes 4 servings

URBAN FARMER CALABACITAS

2–3 tbsp olive oil

1 white onion, diced

2 garlic cloves, peeled and minced

¼ tsp cumin seeds, toasted and ground

4 medium zucchinis, diced

1 large ear of corn, to make 1 cup (250 mL) kernels (fresh if in season, otherwise frozen)

1 large red tomato (or 2 small tomatoes), diced

1–2 jalapeños, minced

sea salt and freshly ground pepper, to taste

1 tsp lime juice

½ bunch cilantro, stems removed and coarsely chopped

1 avocado, peeled, seeded, and sliced

4 oz (115 g) crumbled queso fresco (optional)

This traditional recipe has been handed down from our abuelitas and is a great way for urban farmers to use their summer squash harvest. It's flavorful, satisfying, and full of health benefits. Summer squash is very good for regulating blood sugar; it contains a unique polysaccharide that has been shown in animal studies to prevent diabetes and help regulate insulin. Summer squash is also anti-inflammatory and has anti-cancer properties.

....

In a large frying pan on medium, heat oil. Sauté onions for 5 minutes. Add garlic and cumin and swirl to combine for about 1 minute. Stir in zucchini, corn, tomatoes, and jalapeño and sauté, stirring occasionally, for about 10 minutes or until vegetables are crisp-tender. Taste and season with salt, pepper, and lime juice. Stir in cilantro. Serve immediately, topped with a few slices of avocado and a sprinkle of cheese.

BOOST THE MEDICINE:

Add fresh herbs from your garden when you add the cilantro. Little snippets of fresh oregano, thyme, parsley, pápalo, epazote, or yerbaníz will add complexity and flavor to this dish.

SHOPPING NOTE:

Any summer squash can be used in this recipe. Choose beautiful heirloom varieties at the farmer's market or grow your own. Feel free to mix and match: a combination of yellow and green zucchini looks (and tastes) amazing.

GREENS, BEANS & CHILTEPINES

This is an old-fashioned recipe that we want to reclaim. Our ancestors knew that they could add a punch of nutrition to their beans by combining them with quelites (wild greens). Many variations of this recipe can be found in old, self-published, New Mexican cookbooks. The chiltepin is considered the "grandmother" of chiles, and in the Sonora desert is found growing under mesquite trees. Serve with Mesquite Corn Tortillas (p. 158).

....

In a large frying pan on medium heat, melt oil and add crushed chiles, swirling them in the hot oil. Quickly add onions and sauté until onions are soft, about 4 minutes. Add garlic and cook until garlic releases its fragrance, about 1 minute. Stir in *quelites*. If they don't all fit in pan at once, add a handful at a time and allow them to cook down before adding more. Add ¼ cup (60 mL) water if greens stick to bottom of pan. Continue to cook until *quelites* are wilted and cooked through, about 5–10 minutes. Season with salt. Add whole beans along with some bean stock or a little water. Cook until heated through, about 5 minutes.

1 tbsp extra virgin coconut oil

4 chiltepin chiles, crushed

1 white onion, chopped

5 garlic cloves, peeled and minced

6–8 cups (1 ½–2 L) quelites (lamb's quarters) or spinach leaves, washed thoroughly

½ tsp sea salt

2 cups (500 mL) "Old School Pinto Beans" cooked de olla (p. 151)

CHAPTER NINE
Salsas, Sauces & Toppings

CHIPOTLES EN ADOBO

Many recipes call for chipotles en adobo and most people use the canned version, which is readily available. We've developed this recipe to make our own (without those pesky preservatives). The results are smoky, spicy, and full of zing.

....

On a dry griddle on medium heat, toast chiles for 1 minute on each side, taking care not to burn. Place chiles in a bowl and cover with boiling water. Use a small plate to keep chiles submerged for 30 minutes. Remove stems and seeds, and dip chiles in soaking liquid to wash away seeds.

In a medium saucepan on high heat, combine chiles with remainder of ingredients (except final tbsp of vinegar) and 1 cup (250 mL) water. Bring to a low boil and reduce heat to low. Simmer for 50 minutes, stirring occasionally. At this point, a thick sauce should surround chiles. Allow mixture to cool and finish with 1 tbsp vinegar. Because most recipes call for using 1–2 chiles at a time (they are spicy!), freeze in small containers or small freezer bags, each containing 2 chiles and a bit of sauce.

- 10–12 dried whole chipotle chiles
- 1 8-oz (227-g) can tomato sauce
- ¼ cup (60 mL) Pineapple Vinegar (p. 177) or apple cider vinegar
- 1 small white onion, minced
- 2 garlic cloves, peeled and minced
- ¼ cup (60 mL) raw local honey
- ½ tsp sea salt
- 6 allspice berries, toasted and ground
- ½ tsp dried thyme
- 1 bay leaf
- 1 additional tbsp of vinegar for finishing

makes 1 cup (250 mL)

CHIPOTLE SALSA

Smoky, tangy, spicy goodness! This roasted salsa is a great way to feature your homemade Chipotles en Adobo. The addition of xoconostle, if available, adds a sour-sweet note. If xoconostle is not available, feel free to substitute tomatillos.

....

2 whole plum tomatoes

1 small onion, sliced into ½-in (1-cm) rounds

4 unpeeled garlic cloves

4 xoconostle or 4 tomatillos, husks removed

2 tbsp minced Chipotles en Adobo (p. 167) or canned

¼ cup (60 mL) loosely packed cilantro leaves

½ tsp sea salt

½ tsp lime juice

Heat a dry griddle on high for 5 minutes. Place tomatoes, onions, and garlic on griddle. Cut xoconostle in half, remove seeds, and place on griddle, cut side down. Turn tomatoes, onions, garlic, and xoconostle until slightly charred on all sides, about 5 minutes. Remove skin from tomatoes, xoconostle, and garlic. Place in a food processor and pulse several times to combine. Don't overprocess; salsa should be a bit chucky. Add chipotles, cilantro, salt, and lime juice and pulse to combine until small flecks of cilantro are scattered throughout salsa. Taste and adjust seasonings, adding more chipotle if a spicier salsa is desired.

PICO DE GALLO

Pico de Gallo is a raw salsa that allows fresh, luscious tomatoes and chiles to really shine. It's best made in the summer months with tomatoes from the farmer's market (or even better, homegrown). When tomatoes are not in season, use another fruit, such as mangoes—feel free to be creative. We once made this salsa with honeydew melons, for example, and it was amazing. The key is a sharp knife to make your dice even for each ingredient.

....

In a large bowl, gently toss all ingredients to combine. Taste and adjust seasonings, adding more chiles if a spicier salsa is desired.

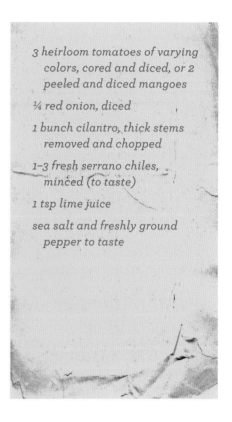

3 heirloom tomatoes of varying colors, cored and diced, or 2 peeled and diced mangoes

¼ red onion, diced

1 bunch cilantro, thick stems removed and chopped

1–3 fresh serrano chiles, minced (to taste)

1 tsp lime juice

sea salt and freshly ground pepper to taste

ROASTED GUAJILLO SALSA

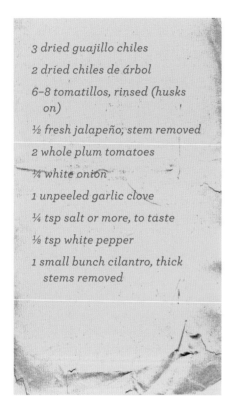

3 dried guajillo chiles

2 dried chiles de árbol

6–8 tomatillos, rinsed (husks on)

½ fresh jalapeño, stem removed

2 whole plum tomatoes

¼ white onion

1 unpeeled garlic clove

¼ tsp salt or more, to taste

⅛ tsp white pepper

1 small bunch cilantro, thick stems removed

Our friend Adilia refers to Luz as tio (uncle). The two spend quality time together, working in the garden, pulling weeds, planting, tending, and chatting. Afterwards, Luz cooks a healthy meal, sometimes with garden ingredients. One evening after working together, Luz made batch of Turnip Green Tacos (p. 136) and Adilia's smoky, roasted salsa was a perfect match for the tacos. This is her recipe.

Heat a dry griddle on medium for 5 minutes. Toast dried chiles for 1 minute on each side, taking care not to burn. Put chiles in a heat-proof bowl and cover with boiling water. Use a small plate to keep them submerged for 30 minutes. Remove stems and seeds from chiles, then put them in a food processor or blender. In a medium saucepan on high heat, combine tomatillos (with husks) and jalapeño and enough water to cover. When water begins to boil, reduce heat to medium, and cook for 10 minutes. Strain and allow to cool slightly. Remove papery husks from tomatillos. Add tomatillos and jalapeño to food processor or blender.

On a dry griddle on high heat, toast tomatoes, onion, and garlic. Turn frequently and cook until charred on all sides. Allow garlic to cool, snip ends, and squeeze out roasted cloves. Add to blender with tomatoes and onion. Add salt and pepper. (All ingredients except cilantro are now in food processor or blender.) Pulse to blend, but don't over-process; there should be some seeds visible, but no big chunks of onion. Add cilantro and pulse until small flecks of cilantro are scattered throughout the sauce. Taste and adjust seasonings.

makes 1 ½–2 cups (375–500mL)

FERMENTED CHILE "HOT SAUCE"

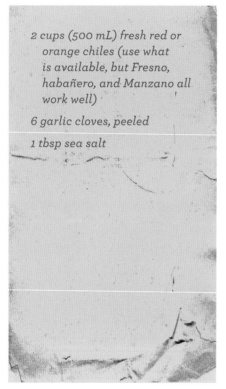

2 cups (500 mL) fresh red or orange chiles (use what is available, but Fresno, habañero, and Manzano all work well)

6 garlic cloves, peeled

1 tbsp sea salt

This sauce is spicy and full of beneficial probiotics. It lasts for months in the refrigerator and is a great way to spice up any dish. Absolutely delicious on eggs and tacos.

....

Trim stems off chiles but leave green caps on as they provide a fruity flavor. Place chiles, garlic, salt, and ¼ cup (60 mL) filtered water in a food processor. Process until smooth. Spoon into a jar fitted with an airlock lid, leaving ¼-in (6-mm) headspace. Seal jar. Store in a dark warm place for 2 to 6 weeks. Remove airlock, stir to combine, place a regular lid on jar, and let flavors develop in refrigerator for a week before using.

CHILTEPINERA HOT SAUCE

makes about 1 cup (250 mL)
—but a little goes a long way!

Chiltepin are wild chiles about the size of a pea. They have a fruity flavor, and while they are quite hot, the heat dissipates quickly, unlike many other hot chiles. The fruitiness of the pineapple vinegar is a perfect complement for these chiles. This recipe produces a very tasty "medium hot" sauce. For a hotter sauce, add up to 1 tbsp chiltepin peppers. This hot sauce is amazing on eggs!

1 dried California red chile, stems and seeds removed

1 tbsp dried chiltepin chiles

1 tsp extra virgin coconut oil

2 garlic cloves, peeled

½ white onion, quartered

½ tsp coriander seeds, toasted and ground

5 allspice berries, toasted and ground

½ tsp sea salt

⅛ tsp white pepper

¼ tsp dried oregano, preferably Mexican

¾ cup (125 mL) Pineapple Vinegar (p. 177) or apple cider vinegar

Heat a dry griddle on medium-low for 5 minutes. Toast California chile for about 1 minute per side. Cut chile into 4 pieces. Place California and chiltepin chiles in a bowl and cover with boiling water. Use a small plate to keep chiles submerged for 15 minutes.

Meanwhile, in a small frying pan on medium heat, melt oil. Sauté garlic and onions for 5 minutes, then add to a blender. Drain chiles and place soaked chiles in blender with coriander, allspice, salt, pepper, oregano, and vinegar. Blend thoroughly for 1 minute or until smooth. Allow mixture to rest for at least 1 minute before opening blender to reduce chance of breathing chile dust.

Decant into a recycled vinegar or hot sauce bottle that has been run through dishwasher or dipped in boiling water. Refrigerate and allow flavors to develop and mellow for 1–2 weeks. This sauce will keep 4–6 months in refrigerator.

SHOPPING NOTE:

Native Seeds/SEARCH (see Sources for Ingredients, p. 239) sells chiltepin chiles that are harvested wild by chiltepineras, women from a cooperative in the Sierra Madre Mountains of Mexico. Chiltepin chiles are also sold in most Mexican grocery stores, either with the dried chiles or in the spice section.

makes 1 ½ cups (375 mL)

RAW GREEN SALSA

8 large tomatillos, husks
   removed

1 small white onion, quartered

1 garlic clove, peeled

1–2 fresh serrano chiles, stems
   and seeds removed

½ bunch cilantro

1 tsp sea salt, or to taste

1 tbsp lime juice

2 tbsp water

1 avocado, peeled and seeded

The raw vegetables in this salsa are full of enzymes that kick-start your immune system. A great sauce for a completely raw meal or a perfect salsa on top of tostadas or eggs, this is the salsa we recommend for our Coyolxauhqui Bowl (p. 113).

....

Place all ingredients in a blender or food processor, and process until small flecks of cilantro are scattered throughout the salsa. This salsa is raw, so it should be refrigerated and used within 2 days.

CLASSIC RED CHILE SAUCE

makes about 4 cups (1 L)

This is the classic homemade red sauce that was served at Luz's grandparents' Mexican restaurant, Las Delicias, in San Fernando, California. It was always used for the Sonora-style enchiladas, one of the restaurant's most popular dishes. This recipe freezes well, so consider making a double batch to save for later. We deviate slightly from the family recipe and thicken our sauce with masa harina instead of wheat flour.

....

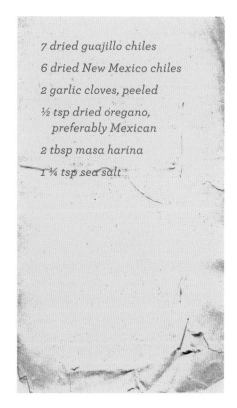

7 dried guajillo chiles

6 dried New Mexico chiles

2 garlic cloves, peeled

½ tsp dried oregano, preferably Mexican

2 tbsp masa harina

1¼ tsp sea salt

Heat a dry griddle on medium for 5 minutes. Toast chiles for 1 minute on each side, taking care not to burn. Put chiles in a bowl and cover with boiling water. Use a small plate to keep chiles submerged for 30 minutes. Remove stems and seeds from chiles and place chiles in a blender. Reserve soaking liquid, straining out seeds. Blend chiles with 4 cups (1 L) water, garlic, oregano, masa harina, and salt at high speed for at least 1 minute, or until very smooth.

Strain blended chile mixture through a medium sieve into a large pot on medium heat. Add 2 cups (500 mL) reserved soaking liquid. Stir to combine. Bring sauce to a slow boil. Reduce heat to low and simmer, stirring occasionally, for 15 minutes, or until sauce has thickened slightly.

makes about 4 cups (1 L)

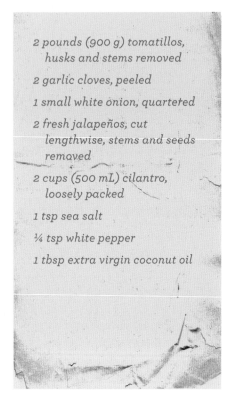

2 pounds (900 g) tomatillos, husks and stems removed

2 garlic cloves, peeled

1 small white onion, quartered

2 fresh jalapeños, cut lengthwise, stems and seeds removed

2 cups (500 mL) cilantro, loosely packed

1 tsp sea salt

¼ tsp white pepper

1 tbsp extra virgin coconut oil

CLASSIC GREEN TOMATILLO SAUCE

In the late 1970s, after a family trip to Baja, Luz's dad developed a recipe for crab enchiladas in a tomatillo sauce. It quickly became a family classic. We have found many different ways to enjoy this tangy and flavorful sauce. We use it in Chilaquiles Verdes (p. 224) and as a bath for our Chiles Rellenos Remix (p. 117).

....

In a saucepan on medium-high heat, combine tomatillos, garlic, onions, and jalapeños. Add enough water to just cover. Bring to a boil and simmer for 15 minutes. Strain and reserve 1 cup (250 mL) cooking liquid. Transfer tomatillos, garlic, onion, jalapeños, cilantro, salt and pepper to a blender. Add reserved cooking liquid, cover blender with a hand towel, and blend until smooth. Be careful when working with hot ingredients! Blend slowly, stop often, and open lid occasionally to allow heat to escape.

In a saucepan on medium-high heat, melt oil. Carefully pour sauce into pan and bring to a slow boil. Reduce heat to low and simmer, stirring occasionally, for 10 minutes.

HOME-BREWED PINEAPPLE VINEGAR

makes about 3 cups (750 mL)

1 large ripe pineapple

Francisco Jiménez, a food artisan from Costa Rica, prepares and sells his raw vinegars at the Phat Beets farmer's market in North Oakland. Phat Beets is a justice-centered farmer's market, bringing real food to working people and providing space for workshops on sustainable food. We attended one of Francisco's workshops where he taught how to make pineapple vinegar using only the ripe fruit. The practice of making vinegar from fruit dates back to ancient times and is something we can all learn. It requires only courage.

....

Top pineapple and remove peel, being careful to remove all spines from fruit. Chop fruit coarsely, including core, and place in a blender. Process for 30 seconds or until no large chunks remain. Place in a large jar. Cover with cheesecloth or any clean piece of cloth. Use a rubber band or string to hold cloth in place. Set in a dark corner for 4–5 months.

Over the course of fermentation, larva or something similar may appear in fruit pulp—don't worry. When it comes time to harvest it, all extraneous matter will be strained out. After 4 or 5 months, pineapple will become vinegar and will be ready to strain and decant. To harvest, pour vinegar through a medium sieve. All kinds of crazy stuff will be strained out. Don't worry, just toss out solids. Strain again, this time through a fine sieve. Strain again several times, now through cheesecloth. Francisco strains his vinegar 7 times to make the finest, clearest, medicinal quality vinegar. After straining, refrigerate vinegar to stop fermentation.

Clockwise from left: Requesón de Semilla de Calabaza (p. 184), Pickled Verdolagas (opposite), Cabbage Curtido (p. 181).

PICKLED VERDOLAGAS

makes 1 ½ qt/L

During late summer months, when verdolagas (purslane) are plentiful, we like to pickle them so we can continue eating them during the fall and winter months. This plant is a nutritional powerhouse. It is higher in omega-3 fatty acids than many other vegetables, protects the liver, and helps heal kidney damage caused by diabetes. You can use pickled verdolagas instead of Pickled Red Onions (p. 180) in any of our recipes as they add a similar acid note.

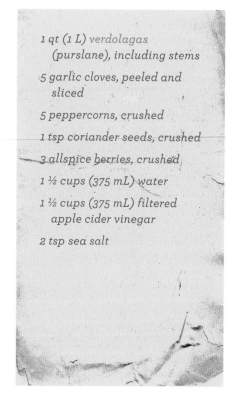

1 qt (1 L) verdolagas (purslane), including stems

5 garlic cloves, peeled and sliced

5 peppercorns, crushed

1 tsp coriander seeds, crushed

3 allspice berries, crushed

1 ½ cups (375 mL) water

1 ½ cups (375 mL) filtered apple cider vinegar

2 tsp sea salt

Pack *verdolagas* into 3 pint (½-L) glass jars or equivalent. In a medium saucepan on high, heat remainder of ingredients until mixture begins to just simmer, about 5 minutes. Pour warm liquid into jars, filling jars to brim. If there is not enough liquid, add more vinegar, straight from jar. Seal tightly and let rest at room temperature for 3 hours. Eat right away or store in refrigerator. Keeps refrigerated for 3–4 months.

makes about 1 ½ cups (375 mL)

PICKLED RED ONIONS

Pretty, pink pickled red onions add a pleasant acidity to heavy spicy dishes. We like to keep a batch of these in the refrigerator. They're not only beautiful on enchiladas, but also complement eggs, salads, and tacos.

....

1 red onion

1 cup (250 mL) apple cider vinegar, strained

1 cup (250 mL) water

1 tsp sea salt

½ small (about 1 oz [30 g]) cone piloncillo or 2 tbsp muscovado sugar

1 bay leaf

4 peppercorns

2 allspice berries

Peel onion and remove ends. With a sharp knife, slice into thin, even rings. Separate rings and place in a heatproof dish.

In a saucepan on medium-high heat, cook remainder of ingredients. Stir to melt *piloncillo*. When mixture comes to a boil, remove from heat and pour over onion rings. If necessary, use tongs to gently move rings around so that they are thoroughly coated with vinegar. Let sit for 30 minutes, tossing rings occasionally. Refrigerate in a tightly sealed glass jar or container.

FERMENTED RED CABBAGE CURTIDO

makes 1 quart (1 L)

Curtido, *like kimchi and sauerkraut, contains healthy probiotics, which are good for the immune system and digestion. Curtido is best known as a topping for Salvadoran pupusas and is generally made with green cabbage. Delicious and beautiful, this red curtido adds a nutritional boost to dishes. We serve it as a garnish, especially for tacos and tlacoyos.*

....

In a large salad bowl, toss cabbage, onions, and carrots with salt. With clean hands, squeeze vegetables until they start to soften and release their liquid (at least 5 minutes). Allow mixture to rest for 20 minutes. After resting, vegetables should have softened somewhat. Squeeze vegetables again, trying to get them to release liquid. Add jalapeños and oregano and toss again, this time using a wooden spoon to press vegetables down. Avoid skin contact, as jalapeños combined with salt will burn! Tightly pack mixture, including any juices, into a 1 qt/L, wide-mouthed canning jar. After adding each spoonful, press down on vegetables with wooden spoon. Let sit 2–3 hours. Using wooden spoon, press cabbage down again several times. If brine from vegetables rises above cabbage, proceed. If not, add filtered water to jar so that vegetables are submerged in liquid. Place reserved cabbage leaf on top of mixture, top with glass marbles, ceramic pie weights, or ceramic pickle weights, and screw on an airlock lid.

1 medium head purple cabbage, cored and sliced into thin ribbons (reserve 1 outer leaf)

½ small white onion, sliced thinly

2–3 carrots, scrubbed and grated on large holes of box grater

1 tbsp + 1 tsp kosher salt

2 fresh jalapeños, thinly sliced

½ tsp dried oregano, preferably Mexican

CONTINUED ▶

▶▶ Store jar in dark corner or cabinet and allow cabbage to ferment for at least 1 week and up to 2 months. Check every few days to make sure vegetables are submerged under brine. If white foam forms on top, just scrap it off; it's harmless. When fermentation is completed to individual taste, remove airlock and seal jar with standard lid. Will keep in refrigerator for 4 months.

We recommend that beginner fermenters use an airlock lid. We have found this a reliable way to ferment. It can help reduce the formation of a white foamy substance that, while harmless, may be unappealing to some. If you don't have an airlock, you can cover the jar with a clean piece of fabric held in place with a rubber band.

CASHEW CREMA

A satisfying, healthy vegan alternative to cheese, this has the consistency of Mexican crema, a tangy loose sour cream that is a popular topping on Mexican dishes. We recommend Cashew Crema in many of our recipes as a vegan alternative to queso cotija and queso fresco. Put some in a squeeze bottle and add as a last-minute garnish to any vegan dish.

....

Place all ingredients in a blender and process until smooth. A high-speed blender works best, but a regular one is fine. Scrape sides often. Keeps refrigerated for 3–4 days.

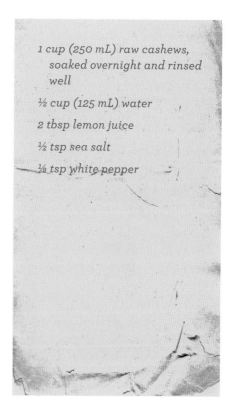

1 cup (250 mL) raw cashews, soaked overnight and rinsed well

½ cup (125 mL) water

2 tbsp lemon juice

½ tsp sea salt

⅛ tsp white pepper

makes 1 cup (250 mL)

REQUESÓN DE SEMILLA DE CALABAZA

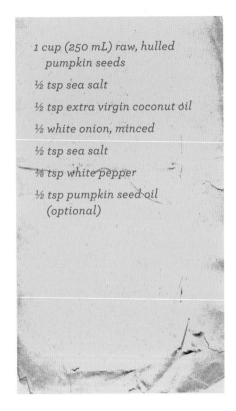

1 cup (250 mL) raw, hulled
  pumpkin seeds

½ tsp sea salt

½ tsp extra virgin coconut oil

½ white onion, minced

½ tsp sea salt

⅛ tsp white pepper

½ tsp pumpkin seed oil
  (optional)

We found inspiration for this dish in a special issue of the journal Arqueología Mexicana that focused on "The Pre-Hispanic Kitchen." This recipe originates in the Sonoran region of Northern Mexico, the birthplace of our grandmothers. Requesón is a ricotta cheese, but this pumpkin-seed ricotta was prepared and eaten in Mexico hundreds of years before the arrival of dairy cheese. It makes a delicious garnish for any entrée, and is a healthy and nutritious snack when served in a warm tortilla. So simple, yet so delicious.

....

Soak pumpkin seeds in enough water to cover and ½ tsp salt for 8–12 hours. Rinse and drain well.

In a small frying pan on medium heat, toast seeds for about 4–6 minutes, shaking pan often. Using a *molcajete* or food processor, grind seeds to a powder.

In a small saucepan pan on medium heat, combine ground pumpkin seeds with 2 cups (500 mL) water. When mixture begins to boil, reduce heat to low and simmer for 5 minutes, stirring often. Remove from heat and add 1 cup (250 mL) cool water. Strain mixture through a sieve lined with cheesecloth. Don't squeeze cheesecloth, as some moisture should remain. In a food processor, blend mixture again or grind in *molcajete*.

In a small frying pan on medium heat, melt oil and sauté onions until translucent, about 4–7 minutes. Add pumpkin seed paste, salt, and pepper. Stir to combine. Reduce heat to low and cook, stirring constantly for 5 minutes to allow flavors to meld and "cheese" to come together. Add water if necessary to prevent burning. Remove from heat. Finish with a drizzle of pumpkin seed oil.

CHAPTER TEN

Postres y Dulces: Sweet Snacks & Desserts

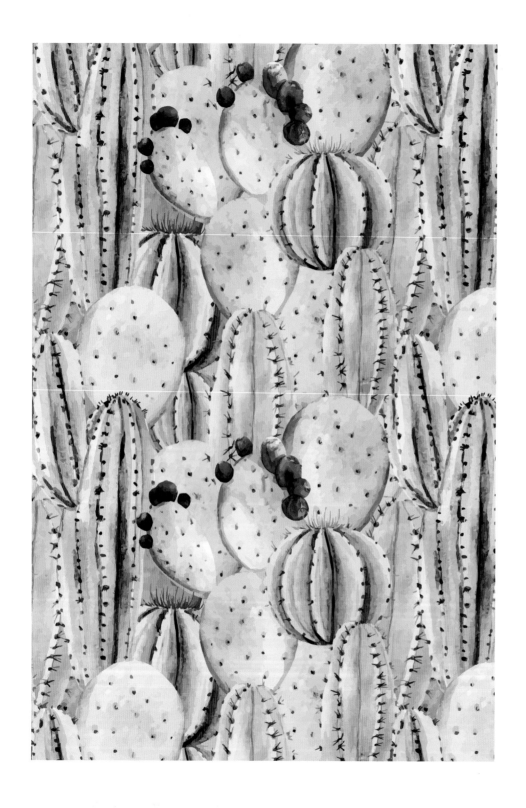

PUMPKIN EMPANADAS

Empanadas are "hand pies," easy to carry for a lunch or snack, and always popular with working people, especially miners. Recently, after some friends were arrested for their participation in a protest march, several friends proposed providing "court support." One person decided to take them coffee, and Luz made up a batch of pumpkin empanadas, a favorite flavor from childhood. The activists breakfasted on coffee, empanadas, and other treats while awaiting arraignment. These empanadas are bite-sized, and we use whole wheat flour to add fiber. Easy to pass around and share.

....

Preheat oven to 375°F (190°C).

In a mixing bowl, whisk together flour, ½ tsp salt, and ½ tsp cinnamon. Using a pastry cutter or fork, cut in butter, leaving some pea-sized chunks. Sprinkle ⅓ cup (80 mL) ice water over dry ingredients and toss. Gently work mixture with hands until dough comes together to form a ball. If dough does not stick together, add more water, little by little. Do not overwork. Cut into 2 equal portions and form into balls and then press down to form thick discs. Cover discs with plastic wrap and refrigerate for 15 minutes.

In a saucepan on medium heat, melt butter. Add pumpkin, sugar, allspice, nutmeg, ⅛ tsp salt, and ½ tsp cinnamon. Stir until sugar has melted and mixture has a uniform color. Continue to cook for 10 minutes on low heat, stirring occasionally. Remove from heat and allow mixture to rest for about 5 minutes.

2 cups (500 mL) whole-wheat pastry flour

½ tsp sea salt

½ tsp ground cinnamon, preferably Ceylon or *canela Mexicana*

12 tbsp cold, unsalted butter (preferably pastured), cut into small pieces

⅓–½ cup (80–125 mL) ice cold water

3 tbsp butter, preferably pastured, or coconut oil

1 15-oz (425-g) can organic pumpkin (not pie filling) or 2 cups fresh pumpkin, roasted and puréed

½ cup (125 mL) muscovado sugar

3 allspice berries, ground

pinch freshly grated nutmeg

⅛ tsp sea salt

½ tsp ground cinnamon, preferably Ceylon or *canela Mexicana*

1 beaten egg (optional)

CONTINUED ▶

▶▶ Place a dough ball on a large, floured cutting board. Use a floured rolling pin to roll out until it is about ⅛ in (3 mm) thick. Using a round cookie cutter or drinking glass (about 3 ½ in [8.8 cm] in diameter), cut dough into circles. Add 1 tsp filling to center of each circle. (Don't add too much or it will be difficult to close empanadas.) With a wet finger, lightly dab water on edges of each circle. Carefully fold empanadas in half and gently crimp edges. Using a toothpick, punch a few holes in each empanada to allow steam to escape.

Place on a cookie sheet lined with parchment paper and brush tops lightly with beaten egg to give them a glossy finish. Bake for 20 minutes or until empanadas turn golden-brown.

CANDIED PUMPKIN

makes 20–30 candies

Luz grew up eating candied pumpkin, which was sold at panaderías and church fairs. This sweet treat is used as an offering for traditional Day of the Dead celebrations. Because indigenous people in Mesoamerica used honey as their primary sweetener, we devised this honey-based recipe. Although the recipe is simple, it does require time, taking 2 days to complete. The slaked lime, also called cal, is used to harden the outside of the pumpkin, allowing it to hold up to long cooking times.

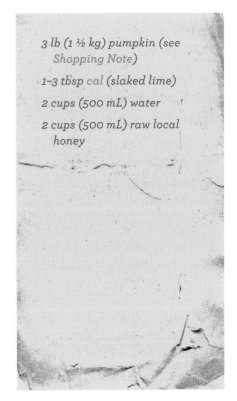

3 lb (1 ½ kg) pumpkin (see Shopping Note)

1–3 tbsp cal (slaked lime)

2 cups (500 mL) water

2 cups (500 mL) raw local honey

CONTINUED ▶

....

Peel pumpkin and cut in half. Scoop out seeds and remove as much of stringy insides as possible. Cut into approximately 2-in (5-cm) squares, rectangles, or triangles; irregular shapes are fine.

Whisk 1 tbsp slaked lime into 1 qt/L water to make a slurry. Place pumpkin in a very large jar or nonreactive bowl and pour slurry over pumpkin, until completely covered. (If necessary, make more slurry.) Cover jar or bowl. Leave pumpkin in slurry for 12–18 hours, occasionally stirring gently as slaked lime will sink to bottom. After soaking, remove pumpkin, drain, and rinse each piece thoroughly.

In a stockpot on high heat, bring pumpkin with enough water to cover to a boil. Reduce heat to medium and cook for 5 minutes. Rinse pumpkin wedges and leave them in a colander to drain for 1–4 hours. With a fork, poke holes in each piece of pumpkin on all sides. Clean pot well, add water and honey, and bring to a boil on high heat, stirring to dissolve honey. Add pierced pumpkin pieces to honey mixture, reduce heat to low, cover, and simmer for 1 hour.

Preheat oven to 300°F (150°C).

▶▶ Spread pumpkin pieces on a parchment-lined baking
sheet. Spoon a small amount of syrup over pumpkin
to lightly coat on all sides. Bake for 2 hours. Place
candied pumpkin pieces on fresh parchment paper
and allow to dry at room temperature for at least
5 hours or overnight. Store in an airtight container in
refrigerator.

SHOPPING NOTE:

*A sugar pie pumpkin will work for this recipe; however, we
prefer to use heirloom winter squash sold at our farmer's
market. Consider using a Cinderella pumpkin (also called
Rouge vif D'Etampes), Long Island Cheese pumpkin, or
Fairy Tale pumpkin (also called Musquée de Provence).*

SWEET BEAN TAMALITOS WITH RAISINS

Sweet tamales are less well-known outside of Mexican communities than their savory counterparts. They are an old-fashioned treat, from a time before cookies and candies could be purchased at every corner market. Because they have a base of whole-grain corn, sweet tamales are easier for our bodies to assimilate than commercial sweets: they contain fiber and protein to balance out the sugar. This recipe comes from Luz's grandmother and features sweetly spiced pinto beans.

....

1. Prepare Filling

In a slow cooker, cook beans in 2 cups (500 mL) water on high for 4–6 hours or on low for 6–9 hours, or until skins are soft and insides are creamy. Add salt to beans after 3 hours but before beans are done cooking. Strain beans, reserving 1 cup (250 mL) pot liquor. In a large frying pan on medium heat, melt coconut oil. Transfer beans to frying pan and mash well with a potato masher. Add *piloncillo*, cinnamon, cloves, and ½ cup (125 mL) reserved pot liquor. Stir to melt *piloncillo*, adding more pot liquor if beans are too dry. When *piloncillo* has melted, add raisins and stir to combine. Taste beans and adjust seasonings. They should be sweet, not savory, and you should be able to taste cinnamon. Beans should have consistency of a thick paste. Cook off liquid, if necessary. Remove from heat and set aside.

Filling:

1 cup (250 mL) dried pinto beans

1 tsp salt

1 tbsp extra virgin coconut oil

2 small cones *piloncillo* (about 1 oz [30 g] each)

1 tbsp ground cinnamon, preferably Ceylon or *canela Mexicana*

1 pinch (about ⅟16 tsp) ground cloves

¼ cup (60 mL) raisins

Masa:

1 cinnamon stick, preferably Ceylon or *canela Mexicana*

1 small (about 1 oz [30 g]) cone *piloncillo*

1 cup (250 mL) non-hydrogenated shortening

1 tsp sea salt

1 tbsp aluminum-free baking powder

3 lb (1 ½ kg) fresh masa for tamales (without added salt or shortening)

3 dozen corn husks, cleaned and soaked in warm water for at least 30 minutes

CONTINUED ▶

2. Prepare Masa

In a small saucepan on low heat, create a sweet cinnamon tea by simmering cinnamon stick, *piloncillo*, and 1 cup (250 mL) water until *piloncillo* has melted, about 10–15 minutes. Strain mixture and set aside. Using a hand or stand mixer, whip shortening for 5 minutes, or until doubled in size. Add salt and baking powder and whip into shortening. Add masa and ½ cup (125 mL) cinnamon tea, a bit at a time. When mixture becomes too thick to beat with hand mixer (if using), hand knead for about 20 minutes. At first masa may be sticky. As masa is worked, liquid will be absorbed and it will become less sticky. When it feels less sticky, put a pea-size piece of masa into a glass of cool water to see if it floats. If it doesn't float, continue to knead or add more shortening or more tea, as needed.

3. Assemble Tamalitos

Set out ingredients (sweet beans, masa), each in a separate bowl. Take a corn husk: notice that it is vaguely triangular and that one side is smoother than the other (which has more pronounced ridges). Lay husk out before you, smooth side up, and base of triangle at top. Place a scant ¼ cup (60 mL) masa on corn husk. With a spoon or fingers, spread masa to create a rectangle about 3 x 5 in (8 x 12 cm) and about ⅛ in (3 mm) thick. Leave a ½ in (1 cm) border at top, ¼ in (6 mm) on each side, and about 1 in (2.5 cm) at bottom. Leave narrow point of triangle entirely free of masa. Place 1 tbsp sweet bean mixture in center of rectangle. Bring 2 sides together, folding 1 side over the other. Fold bottom point up. Tamales are now open at top and enclosed on the other 3 sides. Place in a baking dish, open end on top. Repeat until you have used up either masa, corn husks, or filling.

4. Cook Tamalitos

Use a tamale pot or large pot with a steamer. Add 3–4 in (about 9–10 cm) water. Stack tamales in steamer, open end up. Place a wet dish towel over tamales to keep steam in, and cover with pot lid. Bring to a boil, lower heat to medium-low, and steam for 45–60 minutes. Remove tamales from heat and check one. If it releases easily from side of corn husk, tamales are done. If they appear a bit mushy, cover and let sit for 30 minutes. Overcooked tamales become rubbery, so don't overcook.

XOCOLATAMAL

Luz's chocolate tamales won the prize for "best vegetarian tamale" in a community tamale competition, whose goal was to raise funds for Oakland's Clinica de la Raza. The flavor combination of corn and chocolate is utter magic. These tamales are a show-stopping dessert but are also lovely for breakfast. Serve with hot coffee.

....

1. Prepare Filling

The filling for these tamales is Chocolate Hazelnut Spread, p. 195.

2. Prepare Masa

Using fine side of a box grater, grate chocolate. Alternately, using a food processor, blend chocolate into a fine powder. Set aside.

In a small saucepan on low heat, create a sweet cinnamon tea by simmering cinnamon stick, *piloncillo*, and 1 cup (250 mL) water until *piloncillo* has melted, about 10–15 minutes. Strain mixture and set aside. Using a hand or stand mixer, whip shortening for 5 minutes, or until doubled in size. Add salt and baking powder and whip into shortening. Add masa and ½ cup (125 mL) cinnamon tea, a bit at a time. When mixture becomes too thick to beat with hand mixer (if using), hand knead for about 20 minutes. At first masa may be sticky. As masa is worked, liquid will be absorbed and it will become less sticky. When it feels less sticky, put a pea-size piece of masa into a glass of cool water to see if it floats. If it doesn't float, continue to knead or add more shortening or more tea, as needed. When masa has reached desired consistency, add in grated chocolate and honey and knead to combine.

1 cup (250 mL) Chocolate Hazelnut Spread (p. 195)

Masa:

3 discs (2.7 oz [77 g] each) Mexican chocolate

1 cinnamon stick, preferably Ceylon or *canela Mexicana*

1 small (about 1 oz [30 g]) cone *piloncillo*

1 cup (250 mL) non-hydrogenated shortening

1 tsp sea salt

1 tbsp aluminum-free baking powder

3 lb (1 ½ kg) masa for tamales (without added salt or shortening)

¾ cup (80 mL) raw local honey

3 dozen corn husks, cleaned and soaked in warm water for at least 30 minutes

CONTINUED ▶

3. Assemble Tamalitos

Set out ingredients (Chocolate Hazelnut Spread, masa), each in a separate bowl. Take a corn husk: notice that it is vaguely triangular and that one side is smoother than the other (which has more pronounced ridges). Lay husk out before you, smooth side up, and base of triangle at top. Place a scant ¼ cup (60 mL) masa on corn husk. With a spoon or fingers, spread masa to create a rectangle about 3 x 5 in (8 x 12 cm) and about ⅛ in (3 mm) thick. Leave a ½ in (1 cm) border at top, ¼ in (6 mm) on each side, and about 1 in (2.5 cm) at bottom. Leave narrow point of triangle entirely free of masa. Place 1 heaping tsp Chocolate Hazelnut Spread in center of rectangle. Bring 2 sides together, folding 1 side over the other. Fold bottom point up. Tamales are now open at top and enclosed on the other 3 sides. Place in a baking dish, open end on top. Repeat until you have used up either masa, corn husks, or filling.

4. Cook Tamalitos

Use a tamale pot or large pot with a steamer. Add 3–4 in (about 9–10 cm) water. Stack tamales in steamer, open end up. Place a wet dish towel over tamales to keep steam in, and cover with pot lid. Bring to a boil, lower heat to medium-low, and steam for 45–60 minutes. Remove tamales from heat and check one. If it releases easily from side of corn husk, tamales are done. If they appear a bit mushy, cover and let sit for 30 minutes. Overcooked tamales become rubbery, so don't overcook.

CHOCOLATE HAZELNUT SPREAD

This chocolate hazelnut spread is a rare indulgence. We use it as a filling in our Xocolatamales (p. 193). Our version is sweetened with dates and retains the health benefits of the raw cacao—very high in antioxidants and a well-established mood enhancer. For an easy dessert, make strawberry chocolate sandwiches: Use a strawberry sliced in half as the "bread" and this spread as the filling.

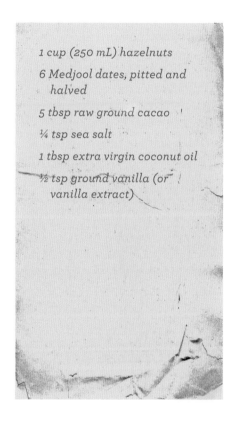

1 cup (250 mL) hazelnuts

6 Medjool dates, pitted and halved

5 tbsp raw ground cacao

¼ tsp sea salt

1 tbsp extra virgin coconut oil

½ tsp ground vanilla (or vanilla extract)

....

Preheat oven to 275°F (140°C).

Spread hazelnuts in a single layer on a cookie sheet and bake for 15 minutes. To remove skins, wrap warm hazelnuts in a clean dishtowel and rest on counter for 10 minutes. Rub back and forth on surface of towel to release skins. (It's not necessary to remove every trace of skin.) Add hazelnuts to a food processor and process until mixture begins to form a butter, about 1 minute.

In a heatproof dish, pour boiling water to cover dates and let stand for 10 minutes to soften. Strain, reserving liquid. In food processor (containing hazelnut mixture), add dates, cacao, salt, coconut oil, vanilla, and ¼ cup (60 mL) reserved soaking liquid. Process until smooth and creamy, about 1–2 minutes. Use immediately or spoon into jar and store, covered, in refrigerator.

5 oz (150 g) bittersweet
chocolate (70 percent
cacao), coarsely chopped

½ cup (125 mL) extra virgin
coconut oil

¾ cup (175 mL) raw local
honey (mild-flavored, runny
variety, such as clover)

½ cup (125 mL) cooked puréed
sweet potatoes

½ tsp pure vanilla extract

4 large eggs

¼ cup (60 mL) raw ground
cacao

¼ tsp sea salt

⅓ cup (80 mL) amaranth flour

6 oz (175 g) fresh raspberries

1 5.4-oz (156-mL) can coconut
cream (not coconut milk),
refrigerated for 24 hours

CHOCOLATE AMARANTH CAKE

This special occasion dessert has the delicate consistency of flourless chocolate cake while also delivering solid nutritional value. The amaranth and sweet potato provide protein and fiber to balance the sweetness of the honey. In addition, cacao may help to prevent heart disease and alleviate depression. This gluten-free recipe, using 100 percent whole foods, is a delicious and healthy way to enjoy chocolate! Because this cake is dense and rich, we recommend serving small slices.

Preheat oven to 350°F (180°C). Generously grease a 9-in (23-cm) spring-form pan with softened coconut oil.

In a double boiler or heatproof bowl set over a saucepan of barely simmering water (make sure bottom of bowl doesn't touch water), melt chocolate with oil, stirring with a heatproof spatula until smooth. Remove top of double boiler or bowl from heat and set aside. Place honey in bowl of an electric mixer and beat at high speed for about 3 minutes, until fluffy. Lower speed to medium and beat in sweet potato and vanilla, then beat in melted chocolate. Add eggs one at a time, beating for 1 minute after each addition and scraping sides of bowl as needed. After last egg is added, beat mixture for 5 minutes (this will add volume to cake). Sift cacao, salt, and amaranth flour into a separate bowl and fold mixture into batter. Pour batter into prepared cake pan and bake for 25–30 minutes, until edges are set but center still jiggles a little and a toothpick inserted in middle comes out with moist crumbs. Place cake on a wire rack to cool for 1 hour. Loosen edges of cake with a knife, then release springform from pan and cool completely before serving.

For topping: Spoon coconut cream into bowl of an electric mixer and whip until it is light and fluffy and holds soft peaks. Serve cake in thin slices garnished with fresh berries and a dollop of coconut cream.

CHOCOLATE PUDDING WITH ACHIOTE

½ cup (125 mL) pumpkin seed milk (see below) or almond milk

½ cup (125 mL) pure maple syrup

1 cup (250 mL) cooked mashed pumpkin or sweet potatoes

1 cup (250 mL) raw cashews, soaked 12 hours in water to cover, drained, and rinsed

½ cup (125 mL) raw ground cacao

1 tsp fresh lemon juice

1 tsp pure vanilla extract

½ tsp sea salt

½ cup (125 mL) extra virgin coconut oil

2 tbsp achiote seeds

1 tbsp kosher sea salt (optional)

We developed this recipe to honor our ancestors who flavored their cacao with achiote. In our research on pre-Columbian spices, we found that before the Conquest, chocolate was primarily consumed as a drink, usually bitter, though often flavored with honey, achiote, or herbs. Our pudding is velvety and creamy, with subtle earthy notes from the achiote seeds. Sprinkle with just a tiny bit of finishing salt to set off the sweetness!

....

In a blender, combine pumpkin seed milk, maple syrup, pumpkin, cashews, cacao, lemon juice, vanilla, and salt. Blend until creamy and smooth, stopping to scrape sides as needed.

In a small saucepan on medium heat, melt oil. Reduce heat to low, add achiote seeds, and swirl seeds in oil for 2–3 minutes, until it turns a deep orange-red. Don't let seeds burn. Strain seeds from oil and discard them. Pour infused oil into chocolate mixture and blend until thoroughly combined. Oil will give a sheen to pudding. Spoon pudding into 6 small cups or ramekins. Cover each and refrigerate for 2–3 hours before serving. Serve topped with a pinch of salt if desired.

Pumpkin Seed Milk

½ cup (125 mL) raw, hulled pumpkin seeds

Soak pumpkin seeds in enough water to cover for 8–12 hours, then strain and rinse. In a blender, process seeds with 1 cup (250 mL) fresh water until smooth, then strain through a fine-mesh sieve or cheesecloth-lined strainer.

TONANTZIN CORN COOKIES

makes 8 cookies

These lightly sweetened corn cookies are our interpretation of a popular street food, *gorditas de la villa,* sold in the area around the Basilica in Mexico City. Cooked on a griddle, these cookies are a quick delight. We add fresh rose petals as our ofrenda (offering) to Guadalupe/Tonantzin, who is known for her miracle of making roses bloom in December. For an original dessert, serve these cookies with Xoconostle in Honey Syrup (p. 201) and garnish plates with a few rose petals.

....

In a small glass, combine tequesquite, baking soda, and water. Set aside to cool. In a small bowl, whisk together honey, egg yolks, and vanilla. Set aside. In a mixing bowl, combine masa harina and butter. Use fingers to work butter into masa harina until it disappears. Strain tequesquite mixture through a fine mesh sieve or cloth to remove impurities. Slowly fold wet ingredients into dry ingredients as follows: add ½ egg mixture and work into dough; add ½ tequesquite water and work into dough; add remainder of egg mixture and work into dough. Add more water, 1 tsp at a time, only if necessary to get dough to hold together. Dough should form a ball and hold together without being sticky.

Stack rose petals, if using, and cut into thin ribbons and then turn to cut into small dice. Gently work rose petals into dough so that there are small specks of petals scattered throughout. Divide dough into 8 balls.

Heat griddle on medium for 3–5 minutes. Reduce heat to low. Press dough balls between hands to form a cookie shape. Place cookies on griddle and turn over after 30 seconds. Continue turning every 30 seconds or so. Depending on heat of griddle, they can cook quite fast, about 1–2 minutes. When lightly browned on both sides, remove cookies from heat and stack on a plate.

- 1 tsp tequesquite or ½ tsp baking soda
- 1 pinch baking soda
- ¼ cup (60 mL) hot water
- 2 tbsp raw local honey
- 2 egg yolks
- 1 tsp vanilla extract
- 1 cup masa harina, preferably white
- 2 tbsp cold salted butter, preferably pastured, cut into small pieces
- 4 rose petals from organically grown roses (optional)

SHOPPING NOTE:

We "borrowed" a few rose petals from a neighbor who does not spray her roses. We didn't take the whole rose, just 4 large petals.

*Left to right: Tonantzin Corn Cookies
(p. 199), Xoconostles in Honey Syrup*

XOCONOSTLES IN HONEY SYRUP

Luz has always preferred sour and tart to overly sweet. This recipe takes the sour fruit of the xoconostle and mellows it in a bath of honey. You can increase honey to 1 cup (250 mL) to temper the sour, or let the fruit rest in the syrup overnight, as it will absorb more of the sweetness.

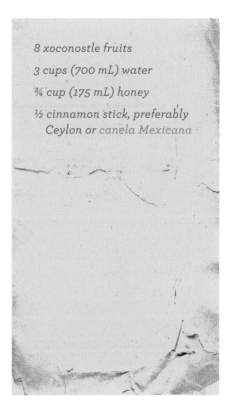

8 xoconostle fruits

3 cups (700 mL) water

¾ cup (175 mL) honey

½ cinnamon stick, preferably Ceylon or *canela Mexicana*

....

Cut xoconostles in half and use a spoon to remove seeds. Using a sharp knife, cut away peel. In a medium saucepan on high heat, bring water, honey, and cinnamon to a slow boil. Gently drop xoconostle halves into boiling syrup. Reduce heat to low and simmer for 20 minutes or until fruit is cooked through. Xoconostle should be tender but still firm. Remove from heat and let fruit cool in syrup for at least an hour.

HERBACEOUS PLUM PALETAS

9 very ripe, juicy plums, pitted

6 yerbaníz sprigs, tied into a bundle with cooking twine

2 tbsp raw local honey (or to taste)

8 yerbaníz flowers

Late June and early July is plum season in our neighborhood. Our neighbors have trees that reach over into our yard and drop red and black plums. Because they all ripen at once, we can't quite keep up with them. Catriona calls this "paleta (popsicle) weather" and developed these plum popsicles as a fresh and fruity way to keep herself cool.

....

In a covered, medium saucepan on medium heat, cook plums, their juices, and *yerbaniz* until plums start to break down, about 20 minutes. Add honey and taste. Fruit should still be a bit tangy. If too sour, add more honey. Remove from heat and cool, covered, for 20 minutes. Remove herbs. In a blender, purée fruit on high speed until smooth, about 1 minute. Remove petals from flowers. Pour plum purée into popsicle molds, adding petals to each mold. Let freeze overnight.

If fresh yerbaníz is not available, use basil or French tarragon and sweet edible flowers such as borage or johnny-jump-ups.

CHAPTER ELEVEN

Bebidas: Beverages

PRICKLY PEAR CHIA FRESCA

makes 1 qt/L

Marathon runners typically carry "power gels" containing fructose and carbohydrates to quickly fuel their bodies during competitions. In pre-Conquest Mexico, runners relied on a natural gel made of water and chia seeds. After soaking in water for a short time, chia seeds change in texture to form a gel. Our lightly sweetened drink is refreshing and rejuvenating.

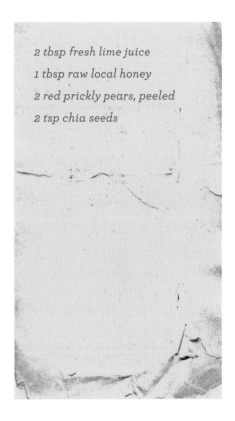

2 tbsp fresh lime juice

1 tbsp raw local honey

2 red prickly pears, peeled

2 tsp chia seeds

In a blender, blend 4 cups (1 L) cold water, lime juice, honey, and prickly pears. Strain through a fine sieve to remove seeds. Stir in chia seeds. Refrigerate for at least 10 minutes to allow chia to gel. Stir again with a long spoon. Serve chilled.

WATERMELON- CUCUMBER AGUA FRESCA

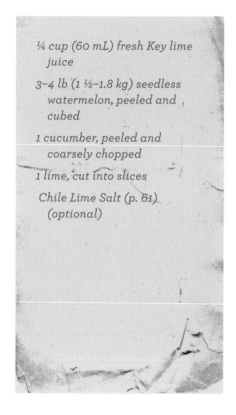

¼ cup (60 mL) fresh Key lime juice

3–4 lb (1 ½–1.8 kg) seedless watermelon, peeled and cubed

1 cucumber, peeled and coarsely chopped

1 lime, cut into slices

Chile Lime Salt (p. 61) (optional)

Beat the heat with this super-refreshing agua fresca! Watermelon and cucumbers act as a natural, gentle diuretic to flush water from your system. This drink is a great treatment for swollen ankles or similar complaints. For a festive flair, rim glasses with Chile Lime Salt and a lime garnish!

....

In a blender, combine lime juice with ¼ cup (60 mL) water. Add watermelon and cucumber and blend until smooth, about 1 minute. Pour mixture into a pitcher along with slices of lime. Refrigerate and serve cold. If desired, rub one slice of lime around rims of glasses and dip rims in a small plate of Chile Lime Salt.

AGUA FRESCA (LITERALLY, REFRESHING WATER):
These beverages are usually prepared with fresh fruit, such as mango, cantaloupe, watermelon, strawberry, or papaya. They are mixed up in large glass jars with lots of water, some sugar, and ice. Aguas frescas are also made from tamarind pods—tamarindo—hibiscus flowers—jamaica— and soaked and ground rice—horchata. Horchata can also be made from pumpkin seeds, peanuts, morro seeds, jícaro seeds, cashews, or barley. Tamarindo, jamaica, and horchata are regarded as traditional "Spanish" flavors, introduced to Spain by North Africans (711–1492). In our recipes, we use small amounts of honey or pilloncillo instead of white sugar as sweeteners.

CANTALOUPE CHAYOTE AGUA FRESCA

This agua fresca relies on the sweetness of the cantaloupe, so it doesn't need additional sweeteners. The chayote adds nutrition, including folate, and is a traditional treatment for diabetes. Cantaloupe may lower the risk of metabolic syndrome, a pre-diabetic condition.

....

In a blender, blend 1 ½ cups (375 mL) water with all ingredients until smooth, about 1 minute. Strain through a medium sieve. Serve over ice, with a slice of lime in each glass.

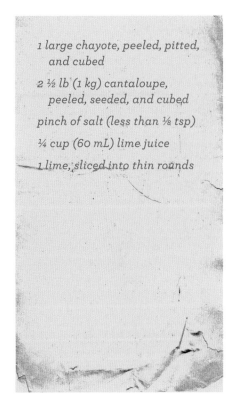

1 large chayote, peeled, pitted, and cubed

2 ½ lb (1 kg) cantaloupe, peeled, seeded, and cubed

pinch of salt (less than ⅛ tsp)

¼ cup (60 mL) lime juice

1 lime, sliced into thin rounds

makes 1 ½ qt/L

½ cup (125 mL) raw, hulled
pumpkin seeds

¼ cup (60 mL) hulled barley

1 cinnamon stick, preferably
Ceylon or *canela Mexicana*

6 cups (1 ½ L) water

¼ cup (60 mL) raw local honey

Homegirl Prickly Pear Syrup
(recipe follows) or Saguaro
Cactus Syrup (see Sources
p. 239)

**Homegirl Prickly Pear Syrup
(makes 1 cup [250 mL]):**

½ cup (125 mL) raw local
honey

4 prickly pear fruits, peeled,
puréed and strained

MESTIZA HORCHATA WITH HOMEGIRL PRICKLY PEAR SYRUP

The word horchata *derives from the Latin word hordeum, a species of grass that includes barley. One origin story says the drink we know as* horchata *was first made of barley. Barley is an ancient grain thought to have been first cultivated in Palestine. Our exceptionally creamy vegan version combines heart-healthy hulled barley and pumpkin seeds. For a unique twist, we recommend serving the horchata with a drizzle of prickly pear syrup, an innovation we learned from Los Angeles chef Pati Zarate.*

....

In a small frying pan on medium heat, toast pumpkin seeds until they being to pop, about 5 minutes. Remove from pan and set aside.

In a large saucepan on medium heat, toast barley and cinnamon stick for about 6 minutes, stirring often. Add 2 cups (500 mL) water, increase heat to high, and bring mixture up to a slow simmer. Reduce heat to low and cook for 10 minutes. Remove from heat and stir in honey. Allow to sit until mixture comes to room temperature, about 30 minutes. Transfer mixture to a blender. If using Ceylon cinnamon or *canela Mexicana*, leave stick in while you blend, otherwise remove. Blend mixture until completely smooth, at least 1 minute. Strain through a fine sieve into a pitcher and refrigerate.

Before serving, to achieve a nice frothy top, pour *horchata* back into blender and blend for a few seconds. To serve, put 1 tbsp prickly pear syrup in each glass and then pour *horchata* on top.

Homegirl Prickly Pear Syrup:

In a small saucepan on medium heat, combine ½ cup (125 mL) water with honey until mixture begins to simmer, about 2–4 minutes. Whisk together. Remove from heat and pour in prickly pear purée. Whisk again and allow to cool. Store, refrigerated, in a lidded jar.

AGUA DE CALABAZA

This drink is inspired by Agua de Chilacayota, a drink made from a squash specific to the Oaxaca region in Mexico. Following chef Zarela Martínez (The Food and Life of Oaxaca), we use spaghetti squash as a substitute, since both squash have a stringy character. Lime twists allow the citrus oil to infuse the drink. It's served ice-cold with strings of squash floating in it. Drink with a spoon if desired.

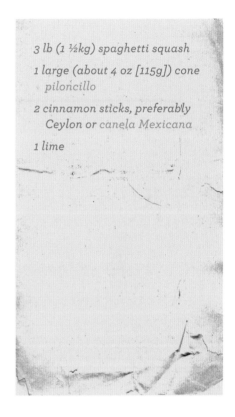

3 lb (1 ½kg) spaghetti squash

1 large (about 4 oz [115g]) cone
 piloncillo

2 cinnamon sticks, preferably
 Ceylon or canela Mexicana

1 lime

Wash outside of squash well. Cut in half lengthwise and remove seeds and stringy center. Cut each half into 3 pieces. In a large saucepan on high heat, bring 2 qt/L plus 2 cups (500 mL) water to a boil. Add squash, *piloncillo*, and cinnamon. Reduce heat to low, cover pan, and simmer for 45–60 minutes, or until squash is completely soft. Remove from heat and allow to cool to room temperature, reserving liquid. Remove squash pieces and gently peel. Use hands to break squash down into strings and return them to the liquid.

Using a potato peeler, remove long strips of lime peel, avoiding pith, from lime. Using a sharp knife, cut each piece into narrow strips, about ⅛ in (3 mm) wide. Twist each strip into a coil and add lime twists to reserved liquid. Transfer to a pitcher and refrigerate for 30 minutes. To serve, place one 1 ice cube in each glass and ladle beverage into glass. Drink will include strings of squash.

makes 4 qt/L

CHICHA MORADA

Chicha Morada is a traditional purple corn drink of the indigenous peoples of the Andes. Purple corn has extraordinarily high levels of phytonutrients and is thought to be protective for colon cancer. This fruity corn punch looks and tastes amazing! Serve hot or cold.

....

1 pineapple

1 lb (500 g) dried purple corn (*maíz morado*) (about 3 cups [700 mL])

¼ cup (60 mL) dried cherries (optional)

½ orange, peeled and seeded

1 tsp whole cloves

2 cinnamon sticks, preferably Ceylon or *canela Mexicana*, broken in half

6 small cones *piloncillo* (about 6 oz [175g] total)

¼ cup (60 mL) lime juice

2 tbsp orange juice

1 lemon, sliced

1 lime, sliced

Wash pineapple well. Remove top of pineapple and discard. Cut off rind and set aside. Remove core and set aside. Dice pineapple and set aside for use as garnish.

In a large stock pot on high heat, combine purple corn, pineapple rind and core, cherries, orange, cloves, cinnamon, *piloncillo*, and 4 qt/L water. Bring to a boil, cover pot, and reduce to a low simmer. Cook for 1 hour. Remove from heat and let cool to room temperature. Strain through a medium sieve. Stir in lime and orange juice.

If serving hot, ladle into mugs garnished with slices of lime and a few cubes of pineapple. If serving cold, transfer beverage to a pitcher, add lemon slices and let chill in refrigerator. Serve over ice, each glass garnished with a slice of lime and a few chunks of diced pineapple.

STRONG WARRIOR NOPAL SMOOTHIE

makes 1 qt/L

During one of our cooking demonstrations in East Oakland, we spoke of the health benefits of nopales, especially for balancing blood sugar. An elder in the audience, an activist whose son was killed by police, told us that when she has a nopal smoothie for breakfast and checks her blood sugar, she finds that she needs only half of her usual insulin dosage during the day. She exemplifies the need to take care of our bodies while fighting larger issues like state violence against communities of color.

....

In a blender, combine all ingredients in order shown and blend until smooth. Taste and adjust lime juice and maple syrup as desired. The sweetness of this drink should come from the pineapple.

½ cup (125 mL) coconut water or water

1 tender nopal paddle, cleaned, spines removed

1 cucumber, cut into large chunks

½ pineapple, peeled, cored, and cut into large chunks

1 tbsp lime juice

pinch sea salt

¼ tsp (just a drizzle) pure maple syrup (optional)

makes 2 cups (500 mL)

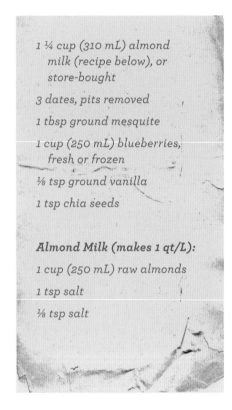

1 ¼ cup (310 mL) almond
   milk (recipe below), or
   store-bought

3 dates, pits removed

1 tbsp ground mesquite

1 cup (250 mL) blueberries,
   fresh or frozen

⅛ tsp ground vanilla

1 tsp chia seeds

Almond Milk (makes 1 qt/L):

1 cup (250 mL) raw almonds

1 tsp salt

⅛ tsp salt

MESQUITE BLUEBERRY LICUADO

The mesquite in this smoothie adds richness, along with protein, fiber, and minerals. The homemade almond milk brings even more protein to this tasty and nourishing breakfast drink, sweetened only with fruit.

....

In a blender, process almond milk and dates until smooth. Add remainder of ingredients and blend again.

Almond Milk:

Soak almonds in enough water to cover and 1 tsp salt for 12 hours. Strain and rinse well. In a blender, combine almonds, 4 cups (1 L) water, and ⅛ tsp salt and blend for at least 1 minute. Strain through a fine-mesh sieve.

FIZZY WATER KEFIR

makes 2 qt/L

It is believed that water kefir dates back to pre-Conquest Mexico, where the grains (tibicos) appeared on cactus growing above 7,000 feet (2,134 m). We like to think of flavored water kefir as a cross between an old-fashioned soda and a champagne cocktail. It is quite easy to make and has quickly become a part of our weekly routine. We especially like the fact that we can experiment and play with the flavors in the second fermentation. And the drink provides beneficial probiotics! Win-win.

....

Note: Don't use a metal strainer or metal utensils as these can injure kefir grains.

In a 2-qt/L canning jar, mix sugar, molasses, and 8 cups (2 L) filtered water. Place water kefir grains in sugar solution. Add 1–2 of the following: dried fig, tbsp raisins, few slices dried apples. (Fruits and molasses add minerals, which along with sugar, feed the kefir granules.) Cover jar with a clean cloth held in place with a rubber band. Let sit on counter (preferably at about 70–75°F [20–24°C]) for 24–48 hours. The longer you leave it, the more sugar ferments out. We recommend 48 hours for fermentation, but don't leave much longer than 48 hours.

Using a mesh strainer or piece of cheesecloth, strain water kefir grains, pouring liquid into another container. Once kefir grains are strained, they can be used to start a new batch or stored in sugar water in refrigerator for use at a later date.

To start second fermentation, put strained, fermented liquid in a glass jar or bottle with a tight-fitting lid or airlock lid. Add flavoring (see suggestions following).

¼ cup (60 mL) white sugar

¼ tsp molasses

¼ cup (60 mL) water kefir grains (see Sources, p. 239)

1 dried fig, 1 tbsp raisins, or a few slices dried unsulfured apples

1 slice lemon peel (optional)

flavoring for a second fermentation, see next page

CONTINUED ▶

▶▶ We find a few small pieces of fruit are plenty, but if we add herbal tea or juice, we use a ratio of about 1:4 tea to kefir water. For additional fizz, add a few tbsp sugar to second fermentation. Cover jar with a tight lid or airlock and allow to sit for 2 days at room temperature. After 2 days, strain out fruit, if necessary, and decant into bottles with tight-fitting lids or flip-top bottles, leaving a little headspace so that bottles don't explode. For maximum fizz, refrigerate finished water kefir for about 24 hours.

Use a large cone piloncillo *(about 4 oz [115 g]) instead of white sugar and molasses. Dissolve* piloncillo *in water, either by heating on stovetop or by placing in blender with water. Allow heated solution to cool completely before proceeding; heat may kill water kefir grains.*

Suggestions for flavoring water kefir using ingredients native or traditional to the Americas:

Lemon Verbena/Strawberry: Soak ½ cup (125 mL) loosely packed fresh lemon verbena leaves in 1 cup (250 mL) boiling water for 30 minutes. Add strained tea and three strawberries to second fermentation.

Hibiscus Flower: Add 5–6 dried hibiscus flowers and ½ lemon to second fermentation.

Prickly Pear: Peel and quarter 1 prickly pear fruit and add with ½ lemon to second fermentation.

Passion Fruit: Scoop out the pulp of 2 passion fruits and add to second fermentation.

Blackberry and Vanilla: Add 5 blackberries and 1 tsp vanilla extract or scrape seeds out of 1 vanilla pod. This will taste like blackberry cream soda!

ALCOHOL CONTENT:

Like kombucha, water kefir is mildly alcoholic, usually between 0.4 and 0.75 percent. Overripe fruit, by comparison, has a similar alcohol content, while beer has an alcohol content of between 4 and 6 percent. A longer ferment will produce a water kefir on the higher end of the spectrum, but still quite low compared to alcoholic beverages.

TEPACHE

Tepache is a fermented drink popular in Mexico, originally made with corn (the Nahuatl word tepiatl means "drink of corn"). Today, tepache is generally made with pineapple rinds, which ferment to produce a tart and refreshing drink. Serve ice cold.

....

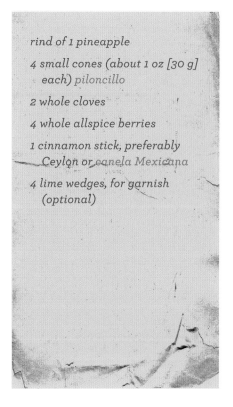

rind of 1 pineapple

4 small cones (about 1 oz [30 g] each) *piloncillo*

2 whole cloves

4 whole allspice berries

1 cinnamon stick, preferably Ceylon or *canela Mexicana*

4 lime wedges, for garnish (optional)

Wash pineapple and remove rind. (Eat or freeze the delicious pine-apple, as you won't be using it in this recipe!)

In a large saucepan on high heat, bring 6 cups (1 ½ L) filtered water to a boil. Add *piloncillo*, cloves, allspice, and cinnamon. Reduce heat to low and simmer, stirring until *piloncillo* dissolves. Remove from heat and let cool completely.

Add pineapple rind to a 2-qt/L jar and pour cooled *piloncillo*-water mixture over it, adding more filtered water if needed to fully cover. Leave at least 1 in (2.5 cm) headspace at top. Cover jar with a clean cloth (such as a tea towel or piece of an old T-shirt) and secure cloth with a rubber band. Store jar in a warm sunny place, either outside or in a window, and leave to ferment for 3–10 days (depending on season and temperature). After third day, check for flavor every day. Tepache should taste tangy. If it's overwhelmingly sweet, it is not yet done. Wait another day and taste again. Bubbles may or may not start to form; either way is fine. When fermented to your liking, strain and place tepache in refrigerator, where it will keep for several weeks. Serve over ice, with a squeeze of lime, if desired.

CHAPTER TWELVE

Desayunos: Breakfasts

BREAKFAST PAPAYA

When we travel to Mexico, we enjoy the opportunity to eat fresh ripe fruit. Licuados (fruit smoothies) are available on every corner, and a simple breakfast of papaya with a squeeze of lime is delicious and refreshing. Mexican papayas are much larger than the Hawaiian variety, and are not genetically modified. The seeds are edible and quite peppery: they make a nice addition to a salad.

....

Wash outside of papaya thoroughly. Cut in half and remove seeds. Peel and cut into large cubes. Divide among four bowls. Juice 2 limes and distribute juice evenly over papaya. Slice remaining lime and use as garnish.

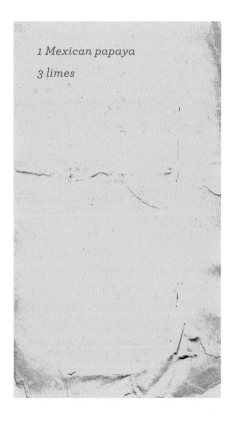

1 Mexican papaya

3 limes

*Left to right: Huevos Urbanos,
Blackberry Atole (p. 226)*

HUEVOS URBANOS

For the past five years, we've been raising chickens for eggs on our urban "farm" in Oakland, California. Our friend Kate built the chicken coop, which we share between two households. We love to see our chickens scampering in the garden, running after a snail or stealing our kale. This dish is a riff on the popular huevos rancheros (ranch eggs). We leave out the fried tortilla and instead serve our eggs sunny side up on a bed of beans and salsa, with warm, soft corn tortillas on the side.

....

In a large saucepan on medium heat, mash beans well and cook until thick and bubbly, 5–10 minutes depending on amount of liquid in beans.

To serve, divide beans into 4 shallow bowls and gently spread them out over center of bowl. Pour ¼ cup (60 mL) salsa over beans and place egg on top of salsa. Season with salt and pepper, to taste. Garnish with cilantro leaves and cheese.

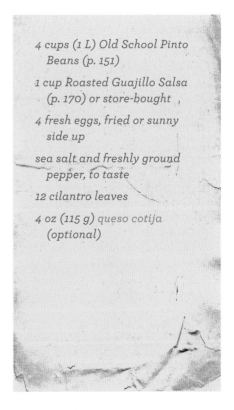

4 cups (1 L) Old School Pinto Beans (p. 151)

1 cup Roasted Guajillo Salsa (p. 170) or store-bought

4 fresh eggs, fried or sunny side up

sea salt and freshly ground pepper, to taste

12 cilantro leaves

4 oz (115 g) queso cotija (optional)

makes 4 tacos

HERB SPIRAL TACOS

The center of our garden is an herb spiral that Luz built out of recycled clay roofing tiles. A lavender plant blooms like fireworks at the top of the spiral, attracting bees to the garden. Below the lavender, Luz grows chives, parsley, rue, several kinds of oregano, thyme, and marjoram. Herbs that need good drainage grow toward the top and those that need more water are planted near the bottom. In the mornings, Luz goes out to the spiral to collect a handful of herbs for these tacos.

....

1 tbsp extra virgin coconut oil

5 eggs

¼ tsp sea salt

⅛ tsp white pepper

2 tbsp mild herbs such as parsley, chives, and/or cilantro in any combination, minced

1 tsp potent herbs, such as fresh thyme, oregano (any kind), marjoram, tarragon in any combination, minced

4 corn tortillas

½ cup Fermented Red Cabbage Curtido (p. 181) or ¼ cup Pickled Verdolagas (p. 179)

4 tsp, or to taste Chiltepinera Hot Sauce (p. 173), Fermented Chile "Hot Sauce" (p. 172), or store-bought hot sauce

In a frying pan on low heat, melt oil. In a small mixing bowl, whisk together eggs, salt, and pepper for at least 1 minute or until eggs are frothy. Pour mixture into frying pan and sprinkle all herbs on top of eggs. Use a heatproof spatula to push cooked eggs to center and prevent sticking. Continue until eggs are cooked through, about 8–10 minutes.

Preheat griddle on medium-high for 5 minutes. Heat tortillas 1–2 minutes on each side. Divide egg mixture between tortillas. Top eggs with curtido or pickled *verdolagas* and hot sauce. Serve immediately.

SCRAMBLED EGG & NOPALITO TACOS

Yes! You can eat cactus for breakfast, lunch, and dinner—it is just that yummy and good for you. Combined with eggs, nopales make a great breakfast to sustain your energy throughout the day. Serve with a side of beans.

....

In a saucepan on high heat, bring 4 cups (1 L) water to a boil. Reduce heat to medium and add nopales. Cook for 10 minutes. Strain and rinse very well. Set aside.

In a large frying pan on low heat, melt butter. Sauté onions and serrano in melted butter for 3 minutes. Add drained nopales and cook for 2 minutes, stirring occasionally. In a small bowl, whisk together eggs, salt, and pepper until frothy. Add egg mixture to frying pan. Use a heatproof spatula to push eggs to center and prevent sticking. After 6–8 minutes, add cilantro and stir to combine. When eggs are just set, remove from heat. Taste and adjust seasonings.

Preheat griddle on medium-high for 5 minutes. Heat tortillas 1–2 minutes on each side. Place a scoop of egg mixture on each tortilla. Garnish each taco with a few slices of avocado and a drizzle of hot sauce.

1 cup (250 mL) cleaned, de-spined, and diced nopal paddles (about 1 medium-sized)

2 tbsp butter, preferably pastured, or olive oil

¼ white onion, diced

1 fresh serrano chile, thinly sliced

6 eggs

¼ tsp sea salt

⅛ tsp white pepper

2 tbsp finely chopped cilantro

6 corn tortillas

1 avocado, peeled, seeded, and sliced

Chiltepinera Hot Sauce (p. 173) or store-bought

makes 4 servings

CHILAQUILES VERDES

12 corn tortillas

1 tbsp olive oil

1 white onion, diced

5 fresh epazote sprigs, chopped
(optional)

2 ½ cups (625 mL) Classic
Green Tomatillo Sauce
(p. 176)

8 oz queso fresco

1 tbsp butter, preferably
pastured

4 eggs

sea salt and freshly ground
pepper, to taste

½ cup (125 mL) Cashew Crema
(p. 183) or ½ cup (125 mL)
crumbled *queso fresco*

½ cup (125 mL) Pickled Red
Onion (p. 180)

½ cup (125 mL) cilantro, loosely
packed

In contemporary Mexican cuisine, chilaquiles are made with corn tortillas torn in pieces and fried in oil. They are a popular (and delicious) way to use stale tortillas, and are often associated with family and home. In our healthy version, we skip the frying. This dish makes an elegant weekend breakfast with friends. Serve with Black Velvet Beans (p. 154) and Colorful Fruit Salad (p. 85).

....

Preheat oven to 400°F (200°C).

Place tortillas on 2 cookie sheets, overlapping as little as possible. Bake for 17 minutes, turning tortillas over at halfway point. Remove from oven and allow to cool. Break each tortilla into about 6 irregular pieces.

In a large frying pan on medium-high, heat oil. Sauté onions and epazote for 5 minutes. Add tomatillo sauce and bring to a simmer. Working in batches, add tortilla pieces to sauce. Stir gently to prevent sticking. Make sure all tortillas are coated with sauce. Mixture may be a bit dry. Reduce heat to low, cover, and cook for 3 minutes. Remove from heat and sprinkle with *queso fresco*. Cover and set aside while you prepare eggs.

In a frying pan on medium heat, melt butter. Crack eggs 1 at a time into a ramekin or small bowl and slide gently into frying pan. Season each egg with a pinch of salt and a grind of pepper. When eggs have set (about 3 minutes), use a spatula to gently turn over. Remove from pan after 10 seconds.

Divide chilaquiles between 4 plates and top each serving with 1 egg, Cashew Crema, a few slices of pickled onions, and a scattering of cilantro.

SWEET POTATO HASH

makes 4 servings

This colorful breakfast hash is our go-to recipe for brunch (and the occasional dinner). We love the sweet and savory notes of the sweet potatoes, red bell peppers, and onions. The tofu adds protein. The hash is full of carotenes from the sweet potatoes: perfect for lifting your spirits on a gray morning. The dripping yolk of a perfectly poached egg spreads sunshine all over your plate.

....

Preheat oven to 400°F (200°C).

In a large mixing bowl, combine sweet potatoes, bell pepper, tofu, and onions. Toss with olive oil, salt, and pepper. Spread mixture on a greased 9 x 13 in (3.5 L) baking dish and bake for 30–45 minutes, or until potatoes are tender.

In a saucepan on medium high heat, bring 2 cups (500 mL) water to a slow boil (water should be just barely bubbling up). Reduce heat as necessary. One at a time, break eggs into a small shallow prep bowl and ease into water. Poach eggs for 4 minutes, making sure temperature of water never comes to a full boil. Serve hash in shallow bowls topped with poached eggs. Season eggs with salt and pepper.

2 sweet potatoes, diced

1 red bell pepper, stems and seeds removed, and diced

1 15.5-oz (439-g) package sprouted tofu, diced

1 yellow onion, diced

3 tbsp olive oil, plus more for pan

1 ¾ tsp sea salt

¼ tsp white pepper

4 eggs

sea salt and freshly ground pepper, to taste

BLACKBERRY ATOLE

1 cinnamon stick, preferably
   Ceylon or *canela Mexicana*

2 cups (500 mL) blackberries,
   fresh or frozen (reserve 4
   blackberries for garnish)

½ cup (125 mL) masa harina

1–2 tbsp raw local honey, to
   taste

Atole (atolli *in Nahuatl) is a warm and nutritious breakfast food going back thousands of years. The Mexica had many variations, some honeyed and some savory. This recipe brings together the anti-oxidant punch of blackberries, the medicinal value of cinnamon and local honey, and the nutrition of nixtamalized corn.*

....

In a saucepan on high heat, bring cinnamon stick in 4 cups (1 L) water to a boil. Reduce heat to medium and simmer for 10 minutes to produce a cinnamon tea. Remove from heat and discard cinnamon stick.

In a blender, purée blackberries, masa harina, and 1 cup (250 mL) water. Pour masa-blackberry mixture through a fine mesh strainer into pan containing cinnamon tea. Put pan on medium-low heat and add 1 tbsp honey. Cook until thickened, stirring constantly, about 5–10 minutes. Texture should be like thin porridge with no dry graininess. Taste and add more honey if desired. Pour into mugs and top each mug with a blackberry.

QUINOA CON LECHE

Inspired by our grandmothers' arroz con leche (Mexican rice pudding), this quinoa and almond milk breakfast pudding is fragrant and flavorful: the protein and fiber give you endurance for your day. Make a pot ahead of time and store individual servings for easy breakfasts throughout the week.

....

In a saucepan on high heat, bring cinnamon stick in 1 ½ cups (375 mL) water to a boil. Reduce heat to medium and simmer for 10 minutes to produce a "cinnamon tea." Remove from heat and discard cinnamon stick.

Place quinoa in a fine-mesh strainer and rinse under running water until water runs clear. Heat a dry saucepan on medium heat, add quinoa, and gently toast it, stirring, until it dries out, about 5 minutes. Add cinnamon tea, lemon peel, and salt, and bring to a boil. Reduce heat to low, cover, and cook for 15 minutes, until all water is absorbed. Add almond milk, maple syrup, and currants. Raise heat and return to a boil. Reduce heat to low and cook uncovered at a low simmer, stirring frequently, for about 15 minutes, until much of liquid has been absorbed but mixture is still loose. Quinoa will continue to thicken as it sits. Remove from heat. Stir in vanilla and remove lemon peel. Let sit for 15 minutes. Taste and adjust sweetness with more maple syrup, to taste. Serve warm in a small bowls sprinkled with cinnamon or portion into small lidded jars and store in refrigerator for quick weekday breakfasts.

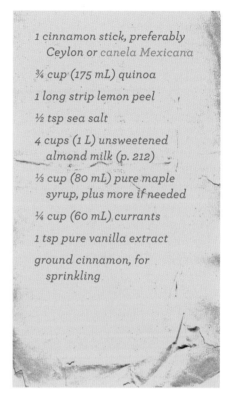

1 cinnamon stick, preferably Ceylon or *canela Mexicana*

¾ cup (175 mL) quinoa

1 long strip lemon peel

½ tsp sea salt

4 cups (1 L) unsweetened almond milk (p. 212)

⅓ cup (80 mL) pure maple syrup, plus more if needed

¼ cup (60 mL) currants

1 tsp pure vanilla extract

ground cinnamon, for sprinkling

CHAQUEWE BLUEBERRY MUFFINS

4 tbsp extra virgin coconut oil

1 ½ cups (375 mL) roasted atole flour, purple corn flour, or blue corn meal

1 cup (250 mL) ground flaxseeds

1 ½ tsp aluminum-free baking powder

1 tsp baking soda

1 tsp sea salt

zest of 1 lemon

3 eggs

⅓ cup (125 mL) raw local honey

1 ½ cups (375 mL) buttermilk

½ cup (125 mL) water

¼ cup (60 mL) extra virgin coconut oil, melted and cooled

1 cup (250 mL) frozen wild blueberries

The first time Catriona ever tasted muffins was when her older sister Christine took a cooking class in high school. Later, when she was in grad school in Colorado, muffin baking was an everyday activity. These blueberry corn muffins are called "Chaquewe cups," in honor of Catriona's dad Alfonso, who says chaquewe (blue corn atole cooked thick and allowed to set up like a bread) is his favorite food from when he was little.

....

Preheat oven to 350°F (180°C) and liberally grease a 12-cup and a 6-cup muffin pan with softened coconut oil.

In a large bowl, whisk together corn flour, ground flax, baking powder, baking soda, salt, and lemon zest. In bowl of an electric mixer, beat eggs and honey on medium speed for about 2 minutes, until lightened. Add buttermilk and water and beat for 1 minute. Slowly beat in melted coconut oil. Add wet ingredients to dry and beat on low speed for 1 minute, or until well combined, scraping down bowl with a rubber spatula. Using rubber spatula, gently fold in blueberries. Fill muffin cups three-quarters full and bake for 25–30 minutes, until edges are browned and they pull away slightly from tins. Remove muffins from pan and cool for at least 5 minutes before serving.

CRANBERRY MESQUITE MUFFINS

This hearty muffin has the desert sweetness of mesquite flour, the protein of corn, chia and quinoa, and the brightness of cranberries. Just ⅓ cup (80 mL) honey brings out all the flavors.

Preheat oven to 350°F (180°C) and liberally grease a 12-cup and 6-cup muffin pan with softened coconut oil.

In a small bowl, combine chia seeds and ¼ cup (60 mL) water and set aside to soak. In a large bowl, whisk together masa harina, corn-meal, quinoa flour, mesquite flour, baking powder, baking soda, salt, and cinnamon. Add cranberries, tossing them in flour mixture, using fingers to break them up. Pour melted butter into a separate bowl and whisk in honey. Whisk in eggs and then buttermilk. Add chia seeds, then add lemon zest. Fold wet ingredients into dry, stirring until just combined. Leave batter to rest for 15 minutes. Fill muffin cups three-quarters full, and bake until golden brown, 20–25 minutes. Remove muffins from pan and cool for at least 5 minutes before serving.

4 tbsp extra virgin coconut oil

2 tbsp chia seeds

1 cup (250 mL) masa harina

1 cup (250 mL) finely ground cornmeal

1 cup (250 mL) quinoa flour, preferably sprouted

¼ cup (60 mL) mesquite flour

1 ½ tsp aluminum-free baking powder

¾ tsp baking soda

¾ tsp sea salt

1 tsp ground cinnamon, preferably Ceylon or canela Mexicana

¾ cup (175 mL) dried cranberries sweetened with fruit juice

4 tbsp unsalted butter, preferably pastured, melted and cooled

⅓ cup (80 mL) raw local honey

3 large eggs

2 ½ cups (625 mL) buttermilk

zest of 1 lemon

makes 15 bars

ALEGRÍA POWER BAR

3 ½ cups (830 mL) popped
amaranth seeds (see
Shopping Note, opposite
page)

½ cup (125 mL) raw hulled
pumpkin seeds

½ cup (125 mL) raw hulled
sunflower seeds

½ cup (125 mL) chopped
peanuts

½ cup (125 mL) dried currants

1 cup (250 mL) raw local
honey

¾ tsp sea salt

¼ tsp fresh lemon juice

We think this is one of the original "power bars." These amaranth treats date back to before the Conquest, when they were shaped into many forms, including skulls, toys, and mountains. Alegrías are sold today as bars or discs in Mexico City's tianguis, or open-air markets. The combination of nuts, seeds, and amaranth make this a high-protein breakfast.
Note: A candy thermometer is used in this recipe.

....

Line a cookie sheet with parchment paper and set aside. In a large bowl, combine popped amaranth with pumpkin seeds, sunflower seeds, peanuts, and currants. In a medium saucepan on medium-high heat, cook honey and salt until mixture starts to foam up. Immediately reduce heat to medium-low and simmer for about 15 minutes, stirring constantly and watching pan so that honey doesn't foam over, until the temperature of the honey reads 300°F (150°C) on a candy thermometer.

Remove from heat and stir in lemon juice. Working quickly, pour honey over amaranth mixture and stir with a nonstick spatula to evenly coat. Spread amaranth mixture onto prepared cookie sheet, place another sheet of parchment on top, and press down firmly to compress mixture. Then use a rolling pin to press mixture into a rectangular slab about 10 x 12 in (25 x 30 cm) and about ½ in (1 cm) thick. With a knife or pastry wheel, cut into rectangles about 4 x 2 in (10 cm x 5 cm) (and save trimmings as a tasty cook's treat). Refrigerate for 2 hours, then wrap bars in parchment paper. Store in an airtight container in refrigerator.

....

SHOPPING NOTE:

Amaranth is sold in three forms: popped, whole, or ground as flour. For this recipe, we're using popped amaranth, and we recommend buying whole amaranth and popping it yourself. To pop amaranth, heat a tall saucepan on medium-high heat until very hot. Add 1 tbsp amaranth at a time, shaking pan constantly until most of it has popped. It takes a while to get the hang of it, but most problems come from not having the pot hot enough, in which case amaranth burns before it pops. When pot is hot enough, amaranth will pop before it burns, at which point you quickly remove it and add the next tbsp. Don't fret if every seed doesn't pop; unpopped ones are still edible.

APPENDICES

MENU IDEAS

Direct Action Planning Meeting

Pachamama Green Salad (p. 78)

Chicana Power Chili Beans (p. 111)

Skillet Cornbread (p. 161)

Cantaloupe Chayote Agua Fresca (p. 207)

Gloria Anzaldúa Reading Group Brunch

Cucumber, Jícama & Mango Sticks (p. 61)

Red Pozole with Medicinal Mushrooms (p. 101)

Borderlands Whole Wheat Tortillas (p. 160)

Mestiza Horchata (p. 208)

Meal for Lovers (or Potential Lovers)

Chicomecoatl Corn Soup (p. 89)

Tacos de mi Corazón (p. 137)

Chocolate Amaranth Cake (p. 196)

Fizzy Water Kefir, Prickly Pear Variation (p. 213)

Harvest Celebration (Autumn)

Sopa de Milpa (p. 95)

Chiles Rellenos Remix (p. 117)

Black Velvet Beans (p. 154)

Pumpkin Empanadas (p. 187)

Tepache (p. 215)

Tamale Party (Winter)

Aguachile de Quinoa (p. 62) & Classic Guacamole
(p. 68)

Red Chile Xocotetl Tamalitos (p. 145)

Butternut Squash & Roasted Green Chile Tamalitos
(p. 143)

Old School Pinto Beans (p. 151)

Tonantzin Corn Cookies (p. 199)

Chicha Morada (p. 210)

Celebrate Spring

Cucumber, Jícama & Mango Sticks (p. 61)

Red Enchiladas Stuffed with Potatoes, Greens &
Pumpkin Seeds (p. 118)

Soldadera Beans (p. 153)

Nopales "De Colores" Salad (p. 76)

Chocolate Hazelnut Spread with strawberries (p. 195)

Fizzy Water Kefir, Lemon Verbena / Strawberry
Variation (p. 213)

Summer Fun

Spicy Salty Peanuts (p. 72)

Verdolagas & Nectarine Summer Salad (p. 82)

Huaraches de Nopal (p. 126)

Herbaceous Plum Paletas (p. 202)

Watermelon-Cucumber Agua Fresca (p. 206)

CONTINUED ▶

▶▶ 5 Weekday Dinners For Busy Schedules

We know you're busy. Follow this plan. The meals build off each other, so it's never a big production.

Sunday: Make grocery list, do grocery shopping, and buy 5 lb fresh masa for tortillas

Monday: Before leaving for work, start Old School Pinto Beans (p. 151). Serve them *de olla* with fresh corn tortillas (p. 155), avocado slices, and Pico de Gallo (p. 169)

Tuesday: Use leftover beans in Tlacoyos con Quelites (p. 141)

Wednesday: Use leftover beans in Coyolxauhqui Bowls (p. 113)

Thursday: Before leaving for work, start a batch of Black Velvet Beans (p. 154). Serve with Sweet Potato Tacos with Red Cabbage Slaw (p. 135) (make double batch of slaw). Make fresh corn tortillas for the tacos.

Friday: Huaraches de Nopal (p. 126) using leftover black beans. Use leftover Red Cabbage Slaw (p. 135).

SOURCES FOR INGREDIENTS

In Your Neighborhood:

Tortillerías: Most neighborhoods with a significant Mexican immigrant population will have a tortillería that makes fresh corn tortillas. This is also where you can buy fresh masa.

Mexican Market: Your best local source of dried chiles, dried herbs and spices, produce like nopales, *verdolagas*, prickly pear fruit, epazote, avocados, and fresh chiles. Some stores will also sell fresh masa.

Farmer's Market: A great source for high-quality, locally produced fruits, vegetables, eggs, and cheeses. Will often sell *quelites*, *verdolagas*, and amaranth greens, in season, and dried beans and chiles. We like to buy our honey at the farmer's market because it's local. Many US farmers markets now accept payment cards and vouchers from SNAP (Supplemental Nutritional Assistance Program) and WIC (nutrition for Women, Infants, and Children) programs.

Health Food Stores: Good source for organic, whole grains, sold in bulk. Amaranth products may be shelved in the gluten-free baking section. Also, often a good place to buy herbs, spices, and raw ground cacao.

Online:

Tohono O'odham Community Action (*tocaonline.org*): white and brown tepary beans, saguaro cactus syrup, *Native Foodways Magazine*

Native Seeds/SEARCH (*nativeseeds.org*): heirloom beans, including tepary beans; dried chiles, including chiltepines; corn products, including blue corn meal, blue corn atole flour, dried pozole (hominy), popcorn; chia; mesquite flour; epazote; Mexican oregano

Mexgrocer.com: Lucia's Herbal Remedies, including chaya tea and mint marigold (*yerbaníz*); organic Mexican chocolate discs; dried chiles, including chiltepin; corn husks for tamales; epazote; tequesquite; avocado leaves; hibiscus flowers; Mexican oregano; *canela Mexicana*; achiote, seeds and ground; *piloncillo*; reasonably priced lead-free clay bean pots; *molcajete*; tortilla press; comal

Bob's Red Mill (*bobsredmill.com*): non-GM masa harina, organic amaranth flour and grain, organic quinoa flour and whole grain, organic chia

CONTINUED ▶

▶▶ Gold Mine Natural Foods (*shop.goldminenaturalfoods. com*): organic masa harina (white, yellow, and blue corn); organic Tarahumara heirloom blue corn; organic beans, including Anasazi beans; organic quinoa; organic amaranth; organic chia; organic pumpkin seeds; dried maitake mushrooms

Rancho Gordo (*ranchogordo.com*): heirloom beans, Mexican oregano (marketed as oregano Indio), dried xoconostle, dried pozole (hominy); *canela Mexicana*; pure vanilla extract

White Earth Land Recovery Project/Native Harvest (*nativeharvest.com*): non-GM dried hominy, traditionally harvested wild rice, maple syrup

Yemoos Nourishing Cultures (*yemoos.com*): water kefir grains (*tíbicos*)

FURTHER READING

Barros, Cristina, and Marco Buenrostro. "Cocina Prehispánica. Continuidad Cultural. Recetario." *Arqueología Mexicana* (no. 12). México, D.F: Editorial Raíces, 2002.

Coe, Sophie D. *America's First Cuisines.* Austin, TX: University of Texas Press, 1994.

Foster, Nelson, and Linda S. Cordell. *Chiles to Chocolate: Food the Americas Gave the World.* Tucson, AZ: University of Arizona Press, 1992.

Jacobs, Martin, and Beverly Cox. *Spirit of the Earth: Native Cooking from Latin America.* New York: Stewart, Tabori and Chang, 2001.

Kavasch, E. Barrie. *Enduring Harvests: Native American Foods and Festivals for Every Season.* Old Saybrook, CT: Globe Pequot Press, 1995.

LaDuke, Winona. *All Our Relations: Native Struggles for Land and Life.* Cambridge, MA; South End Press;, 1999.

———. *Recovering the Sacred: The Power of Naming and Claiming.* Cambridge, MA: South End Press, 2005.

Mihesuah, Devon Abbot. *Recovering Our Ancestor's Gardens: Indigenous Recipes and Guide to Diet and Fitness.* Lincoln, NB: University of Nebraska Press, 2005.

Montoya, Michael J. *Making the Mexican Diabetic: Race, Science, and the Genetics of Inequality.* Berkeley, CA: University of California Press, 2011.

Nabhan, Gary Paul. *Gathering the Desert.* Tucson, AZ: University of Arizona Press, 1985.

———. *Coming Home to Eat: The Pleasures and Politics of Local Foods.* New York: W. W. Norton & Company, 2002.

Nelson, Melissa K., ed. *Original Instructions: Indigenous Teachings for a Sustainable Future.* Rochester, VT: Bear & Company, 2008.

Terry, Bryant. *Afro-Vegan: Farm-Fresh African, Caribbean & Southern Flavors Remixed.* Berkeley, CA: Ten Speed Press, 2014.

Tohono O'odham Community Action with Mary Paganelli Votto and Frances Sallie Manuel. *From I'itoi's Garden: Tohono O'odham Food Traditions.* Tohono O'odham Nation, AZ: 2010. Available online at: *blurb. com/books/3232576-from-i-itoi-s-garden.*

INDEX OF NATIVE INGREDIENTS

ACKNOWLEDGMENTS

We are grateful to share this project with you. We acknowledge the much larger group of people who are re-indigenizing food ways and reminding us of the agricultural knowledge and innovation of indigenous peoples throughout both North and South America. In particular, we owe a debt of gratitude to Devon Abbott Mihesuah, whose book *Recovering Our Ancestor's Gardens* has informed our project. She coined the term "Decolonizing Our Diets" in 2003. We have learned much from the work of Native activists, writers, historians, and chefs, especially Winona LaDuke, Melissa K. Nelson, Chef Nephi Craig, Chef Lois Ellen Frank, Chef Walter Whitewater, and Chef Sean Sherman. The Decolonizing Diet Project, an initiative at Northern Michigan University Center for Native American Studies, has put the principles of valuing local native foods into practice. The group Tohono O'odham Community Action, whose way of confronting diabetes by fighting it with traditional native foods of the desert, sets a very high bar. Claudia Serrato and Chris Rodriguez inspired us early on through their blog Decolonial Food for Thought. We appreciate Phat Beets Produce, whose vision of food justice includes decolonization. We are inspired by many artists connecting Mesoamerican foods with contemporary Chicana/o culture and are especially grateful that Veronica Pérez, Ernesto Yerena Montejano, Melanie Cervantes, Jesus Barraza, and Orlando Arenas have permitted us to use their images in this book. In 1996, we were both students in Emma Pérez's seminar "Decolonizing Queer Theory," and her teachings inform this project.

We are grateful to our community of friends, especially "Mar" San Martín for her masterful editing and thoughtful comments on the opening chapters; Hadas and Margo Rivera-Weiss for generously testing recipes and offering feedback and tips; Adilia Torres for her spirit, her help in the garden, and for being part of our lives; Amelia Montes for conversations, tastings, and brainstorming as she shares her dance with diabetes and embraces new ways of living; Victor Carrillo and Marta López-Garza for their steadfast friendship over decades and for testing our chaya recipe with chaya they grew in their garden; Yolanda Mora and Yolanda Loera for their love and support; and Joe Hopper and Paul Chasnoff who taught Catriona that grownups cook their own gourmet meals from scratch and eat real butter. So many more of our friends and students contributed recipe ideas; passed along tips, leads, and knowledge; gifted us small press cookbooks from travels; and shared food memories and photos of fabulous native foods that we then tried to replicate. This has truly been a collective effort and we are humbled by our friends' willingness to share.

Our families have played significant roles in this project.

We especially want to recognize Luz's dad, Tony H. Calvo (1935–2008) who put so much love into cooking for our family. This book is his legacy. Luz's mom Beverley has tasted many of our recipes and given useful feedback, but most of all provided appreciation and support. Luz's brother Andrew has participated in keeping the Calvo tamale tradition alive by bringing his extended family to our holiday celebrations. Catriona's dad José Alfonso shared his stories about growing up in New Mexico and his mother's garden and her cooking. Her mom, Eleanor, who would rather be outside painting landscapes than inside cooking, has provided great enthusiasm for our work. Catriona's sister, Christine, has taught many lessons about cooking and life, and her husband Salómon, who cooks many of the dinners in the family, has shared his mother's recipes. We're both excited to see the younger generations taking up family recipes: Steven, Cisco, Sal, and Maria.

We are grateful to our students at Cal State East Bay and San Francisco State, who have responded to our project by bringing their own stories, histories, and recipes. This project is inspired by their desire to connect to their ancestors and to reclaim their health. We are grateful to reside in Oakland, where there is a vibrant community of political and spiritual activism that has informed this project. Luz thanks her Decolonize Oakland comrades, especially Yvonne, Al, Rebecca, Irina, Nico, Leo, and Darshan. We appreciate Calpulli Coatlicue and especially Teresa, Ernesto, and Frank, who welcomed us to their spiritual practice and taught us to dance our prayers, and that the oldest stories are of food.

We thank Bryant Terry, for his generous spirit and support of our project, for sharing cookbooks and advice, and for the way the ancestors speak through his books. Thanks to Leda Sheintaub who provided vital assistance with recipe proofing. Lastly, we thank the folks at Arsenal Pulp Press, for embracing all the aspects of this project: cookbook, tradition, teaching, and art: Brian Lam, Robert Ballantyne, Cynara Geissler, Gerilee McBride, Tracey Kusiewicz, and especially Susan Safyan for finding and believing in our project.

INDEX

LUZ CALVO and CATRIONA RUEDA ESQUIBEL are professors at Cal State East Bay and San Francisco State University respectively. Their popular website and Facebook page for "Decolonize Your Diet" promote the health benefits of indigenous Mexican-American cooking. They raise chickens and grow fruits, vegetables, and herbs on their small urban farm, as they study traditional Mesoamerican cuisine and work to create sustainable relationships in their community. This is their first book.